HOW THE USE OF MARIJUANA WAS CRIMINALIZED AND MEDICALIZED, 1906-2004

A Foucaultian History of Legislation in America

HOW THE USE OF MARIJUANA WAS CRIMINALIZED AND MEDICALIZED, 1906-2004

A Foucaultian History of Legislation in America

Jeffrey Matthew London

With a Foreword by
Robert M. Regoli

The Edwin Mellen Press
Lewiston•Queenston•Lampeter

Library of Congress Cataloging-in-Publication Data

London, Jeffrey Matthew.
  How the use of marijuana was criminalized and medicalized, 1906-2004 : a
Foucaultian history of legislation in America / Jeffrey Matthew London ; with a
foreword by Robert M. Regoli.
      p. cm.
  Includes bibliographical references and index.
  ISBN-13: 978-0-7734-3772-2
  ISBN-10: 0-7734-3772-X
  1. Marijuana--Therapeutic use--United States--History. 2. Marijuana--Law and
legislation--United States--History. 3. Marijuana--United States--History. I. Title.
  RM666.C266L66 2010
  615'.32345--dc22

                              2009045920

hors série.

A CIP catalog record for this book is available from the British Library.

Front cover: Photo of marijuana leaves courtesy of iStockphoto LP (iStockphoto.com)

The Edwin Mellen Press   The Edwin Mellen Press
           Box 450   Box 67
     Lewiston, New York   Queenston, Ontario
      USA 14092-0450   CANADA L0S 1L0

                     The Edwin Mellen Press, Ltd.
                      Lampeter, Ceredigion, Wales
                     UNITED KINGDOM SA48 8LT

                   Printed in the United States of America

This one is for my mom, my wife, and my daughter.

In truth, it was my mom who taught me how to live and it was my wife who taught me how to love. But, it was my daughter who taught me how to have fun again.

Contents

Figures

Foreword

In his book on the past and present histories of Marijuana, Jeffrey London takes the reader on a journey through the complicated morass surrounding the criminalization and medicalization of marijuana in the United States. London's fluid and story-telling writing style makes the book a pleasure to read, while at the same time providing the reader with the intricate and subtle details surrounding this topic.

What makes London's book exceptional is that he provides a thorough qualitative historical analysis of marijuana's past and present social constructions. By detailing the way a plant is transformed into a crime, and how a crime is transformed into a medicine, London redefines the traditional debate surrounding the medical use of marijuana. To his credit, his analysis reveals policy alternatives that are hiding in plain sight. As a result, the work breaks the gridlock of the traditional partisan pitch which surrounds the current contest over marijuana regulation. The results of London's study are surprising and are in part the outcome of the method that drives the work.

London adopts a Foucaultian problem based approach (rather than period based approach) to assemble a qualitatively general (as apposed to total) historical examination. The approach London uses is grounded in the writings of the twentieth century French philosopher, Michel Foucault (1926-1984). By excavating the conflicting public policy implications of rival moral paradigms, the study associates sociological theory and cutting edge methods, along with all of the accoutrements of a hot button topic like the marijuana debate.

Throughout London's investigation, two different but structurally identical forms of processual discourse are dissected as the objects of his study. The first processual discourse that undergoes scrutiny is the criminalization of marijuana, which exhumes the past history of America's successful federal legislative initiatives

i

to prohibit the plant. The second processual discourse that undergoes scrutiny is the medicalization of marijuana, which assesses today's history of America's very successful medicinal marijuana movement. Throughout the study, London uses the theory of medicalization as a guide, while putting the Foucaultian method to work to create two histories of one plant. The outcome is a theoretically driven study that illustrates the structural characteristics of each discursive complex. Most importantly, the results of London's analysis illustrate the way by which coercive discursive formations successfully drive past and contemporary deviant designation change. Consequently, London artfully dissipates the fog of the present, shedding light on a topic that is currently in the conceptual dark.

In short, London's study assesses and connects divergent theoretical perspectives to create a holistic and more balanced (i.e., apolitical) investigation. In an effort to further understanding of how the different processes of criminalization and medicalization are employed by the state to regulate the behavior of its citizens, London not only surprises his reading audience with the results, he surprises himself. London's study is not propelled by *what* he is looking for. His study is driven by *how* to look. In doing the unexpected, he accomplishes the unexpected. He demystifies the way by which different processual entities impact the state subjectivity of all patients and criminals. In addition, he unveils the markedly different outcomes for all citizens that experience the impact of either label (criminal or patient). A major conclusion from London's clearly written book is that the employment of a newly reconstructed method and theory displays potential for the advancement of our understanding of the way by which new definitions and new deviant designations successfully emerge over time and become sovereign.

This book makes an important contribution to the scholarly literature on the topic. Presently, there is no substantive equivalent on the contemporary U.S. drug policy debate. The contemporary topic of marijuana medicalization is now ripe for picking. As contemporary marijuana users are increasingly relabeled by successful state level drug policy ballot initiatives, millions of Americans are being redefined by the state, from "criminals" to "patients," particularly under President Obama's treatment approach to drug policy.

In a judicious fashion, London's work patently reveals the way by which two examples of processual discourse (i.e., the criminalization and medicalization of marijuana) reflect and illustrate the way by which deviant designations change overtime, and definitions associated with each distinct discursive complex becomes historically specific. Consequently, he demonstrates to his audience how the "truth" brand of each discourse is only allowed into the real as an associate to its specific and temporal accident of location. Hence, the palatability of specific statements (i.e., definitions of "criminal" or "patient") for the general public are reliant upon specific temporal and spatial locations as they take place in conjunction with specific contingencies stumbled upon by accident.

By fragmenting the reader's preconceived biases, London encourages his audience to think in a new way about the old and stagnant debate. London brings into view the surfaces by which past and present statements occur; as conducive, hostile or inconsequential to the production and subsequent reproduction of statements associated with either deviant designation. In other words, truths and lies take on equal import throughout the analysis. Through specific surfaces, potentialities emerge, quickly fade away or prosper as replications are annihilated, held indeterminately or subsequently privileged into production and reproduction. In this manner, London's analytical histories surprisingly favor neither left nor right.

With processual discourse as the unit of analysis and marijuana as the topic of interest, London assesses the explanatory power of sociological, criminological and postmodern theory by putting to work a prescriptive method. On top of a theoretically and methodologically solid foundation, London produces his analysis through mining an impressively diverse and inclusive set of data. Following a thorough examination of the multiple data sources, London concludes that both examples of process are identical and only differ in arriving at separate deviant definition destinations (i.e., "criminal" or "patient") within the larger arena of the closed and sovereign discourse of state sanction subjectivity. In other words, for London, the newest industry of deviant designation production is structurally no different than the old. In the end, London's book has produced a much better historical analysis than has any other book presently available. When all accoutrements of human interaction are analytically stripped away, nothing more than a simple plant is uncloaked. The fact is that marijuana is a plant; it is not a crime.

What makes London's book good and essential will not be obvious to casual readers; for London's most valuable contribution is the introduction of a new theoretical roadmap for other scholars to follow. By connecting portions of three existing analytical devices, he facilitates the study of deviant designation change on three different levels of analysis (i.e., micro, mid-level, and macro). The first part is a slight variant of *the theory of medicalization*, which is connected to a second part. The second part or the five principles of the *science of discipline* represent the writings of Michel Foucault. Lastly, the third part of the theoretical device is based on Elliot Currie's four characteristics of *elaborate machinery for deviant production*. The resulting theoretical roadmap assists researchers' interested in implementing enhanced investigations for historically specific objects of past and present qualitative historical inquiry. The newly proposed theoretical approach will guide researchers in their study of the "epidemics of immorality" for years to come. Simply put, London has provided us with a groundbreaking analysis that will soon become a must read for all who are serious students of deviance designation change. Bravo, Professor London. By daring to tread off the beaten path, you have advanced our understanding of a critical issue of contemporary society. For that you must be honored and applauded.

Robert M. Regoli, Professor
University of Colorado

Acknowledgments

No undertaking of this kind can come to completion without the effort and support of numerous individuals. In truth, my manuscript and my career would never have seen the light of day without the gracious help of Robert Regoli, Jules Wanderer, Matt Delisi, Dennis Blewitt, and George Rivera. Other colleagues and friends who selflessly gave of their time to provide me with much needed guidance and encouragement include Karl Kunkel, Jeff Nash, Melody Lehnerer, Karen Parker, Jeff Ross, Gary Brinker, Jacquelynn Willard, Sylvia Macey, Laura Jordan, Patricia Shultz, Andrew Catterall, Sandra Haynes, Lying Li, Allison Cotton, John Galliher, Adina Nack, Ronald Akers, Greg Barack, Raymond Michalowski, Randall G. Shelden, Leslie Irvine, Gavin Kendall, Gary Wickham, Danielle Dirks, Emily Troshynski, Rita Shah, David Rohm, Anjuli Verma, Mike Radelet, Frank Barber, Burke Grandjean, Laurel Parker-West, Joanne Belknap, Megan Webb, Sara Steen, Janel Blanchard, Jason Boardman, Rodney Wambeam, Jon Resh, Jay Watterworth, Lonn Lanza-Kaduce, and Dawn Blanchard.

Chapter One

Introduction

In 1992, Peter Conrad and Joseph Schneider published *Deviance and Medicalization*, where they explored how policy and lawmakers categorize and re-categorize societal problems under the labels of deviance, sickness, madness or "badness." Conrad and Schneider's medicalization theory has been used for a variety of issues including compulsive gambling (Rossol, 2001), ADHD adults (Lloyd, 1999; Rafolovich, 2001), racism (Wellman, 2000), welfare (Schram, 2000), grief (Walter, 2000), adolescence (Gillies, 2000), unhappiness (Dworkin, 2001), Type A personalities (Riska, 2000), and erectile dysfunction (Carpiano, 2001). In the broadest sense, this study builds on this body of literature by addressing yet another societal problem that is undergoing a deviant designation change, the medicalization of marijuana.

Conrad and Schneider's medicalization theory provides a starting point for social scientists interested in the study of deviance. By understanding how competing interest groups struggle to have their specific designations of deviance accepted, social scientists might develop a greater appreciation of the political implications of their research. In that regard, this research contends that deviant behaviors are medicalized in the same way that deviant behaviors are criminalized, through a similar process of social construction. More specifically, the focus of this historical analysis is on the criminalization and medicalization of marijuana and those who use it for one reason or another.

Beginning in the early 1900s, there were accelerating attempts by government officials and other powerful individuals to define marijuana use as a criminal problem. Consequently, throughout most of the twentieth century, the

1

production, distribution, and consumption of medicinal or recreational marijuana became the responsibility of the criminal justice system to eradicate. In 1996, governmental efforts to regulate marijuana use began to change in a very dramatic fashion.

Beginning in 1996, several non-profit grassroots organizations started to organize, introduce, and successfully pass medicinal marijuana decriminalization initiatives at the state level. By year-end 2004, eleven states had passed laws decriminalizing the use of medical marijuana for patients with prescriptions written by physicians. As a result, the medicinal marijuana movement emerged as a high profile and hot topic issue within the arenas of medical sociology and criminology.

In spite of the new legislation, federal law continues to prohibit the use of marijuana, regardless of circumstances. Therefore, the medical marijuana laws of the states remain unstable as long as the federal government continues to classify marijuana as a Schedule I drug (i.e., a substance officially defined as a drug with no medical value). The disjuncture between state medical marijuana decriminalization and federal prohibition is the contemporary battleground whereby "moral entrepreneurs" (i.e., the Supreme Court, Bush Administration, ACLU, grass-roots marijuana activists, physicians, and the critically ill) compete for the production of legislative majorities and officially recognized definitions (Becker, 1963). The statements generated by both sides of the marijuana debate are the data for this project.

This book examines how the label of deviant applies to marijuana users over the last 100 years. Data for three unique sets of events are examined. These events were selected because of their close relationship with changes in the official deviant designations associated with marijuana. The data are organized in the following way:

1.   The first set of data is associated with the eight federal legislative acts that resulted in the criminalization of marijuana (1906 to 1986).

2. The second data set describes the laws of the first nine states that decriminalized the use of medical marijuana (1996 to 2004).

3. The third set of data analyzes three recent Court cases on the topic, clarifying the authority of federal government to prohibit marijuana in states that have decriminalized the use of medicinal marijuana.

The data are a collection of state laws, Supreme Court cases, final legislation, legislative records, transcripts of legislative hearings, major newspaper articles, congressional debates, speeches, select committee and subcommittee minutes, evidence and reports of Washington based non-profit organizations, periodical and professional journals, newsletters, biographies, pamphlets, on-line postings, newspaper editorials, letters of solicitation and public memorandums, as well as other amateur and professional literature associated with the criminalization and medicalization of marijuana.

Stages of Deviant Designation

Medicalization theory is used here to investigate the criminalization of deviance in the same way that scholars have used Conrad and Schneider's theory to study the medicalization of deviance. Michel Foucault's five principles of the "Science of Discipline" (discussed in Chapter Two) are used to bridge the conceptual gap between Conrad and Schneider's micro-level tenets and a mid-range analysis that explains how new deviant designations become institutionalized. Finally, Elliot Currie's (1968) macro-level tenets are used to explain how deviant designations, once institutionalized, may or may not enter into a phase of deviant label creation that is uncontrollable and destructive to the social order. After connecting the analytical frameworks of Conrad and Schneider, Foucault, and Currie, the utility of reframing these perspectives as the three stages of deviant designation change are discussed.

Micro-level Analysis

The first stage of deviant designation change uses Conrad and Schneider to examine how a new deviant designation can successfully emerge into a suitable historical setting. While medicalization theory explains the creation of a new deviant designation, the theory is restricted to a micro-level of analysis. It does not explain how citizens learn to accept a new deviant designation. For example, Conrad and Schneider indicate that the final sequence associated with any deviant designation change involves the institutionalization of the deviant designation; however, they do not specify the conditions by which the public embraces new labels such as medical marijuana patient.

Mid-range Analysis

Foucault's principles provide a mid-range analytical guide, which specifies how large bureaucratic institutions (i.e., prisons, hospitals, universities or armed forces) individualize and standardize their own process of socialization. By using programming initiatives, a new deviance designation can gain acceptance and legitimacy. By connecting Conrad and Schneider to Foucault, this study aids our understanding of how a new complex of knowledge (e.g., medical marijuana) can produce new institutionally approved programs, dramatically changing the behaviors of citizens through utilizing new definitions of inappropriate and appropriate behavior.

Macro-level Analysis

While Conrad and Schneider describe where deviant designations originate from, and Foucault's principles specify how the institutionalization of individual behaviors occurs, Currie's work illustrates how criminal designations become prolific. In 1968, Currie put forth a conceptual framework that specifies deviance management techniques. Currie's four macro-level characteristics of "an enormously effective machine for the systematic and massive production of confessed deviants" are discussed in Chapter Two (Currie, 1968: 351). The characteristics illustrate a particular type of social control structure that can result in extremely high rates of deviance. Currie's work describes the characteristics of system of repressive control that bears a striking resemblance to America's system of marijuana prohibition (Currie 1968: 350).

Connecting Conrad and Schindler, Foucault and Currie

In sum, portions of three analytic perspectives are connected to form a framework for studying deviance designation change. The goal of this study is to inspire others to construct theories of their own, which will promote dialogue and discourse.

Kendall and Wickham's Method

Kendall and Wickham's (2000) Foucaultian method is a relatively new qualitative approach to data collection and analysis. The method's namesake is the now-famous French postmodern scholar Michel Foucault whose work inspired Gavin Kendall and Gary Wickham to develop their prescriptive method. Some refer to the methodology of Foucault's contemporary masterpiece, *The Archaeology of Knowledge* (1972), as "unmethodological" or as a parody of a traditional modernist methodological text (Megill, 1985). On the contrary, Kendall and Wickham (2000: vii) contend that their Foucaultian method is valid, and should be acknowledged as a legitimate methodological approach to historical analysis. Both authors situate their method alongside well-established methodological approaches (i.e., textual analysis, observation, and historical inquiry). However, other scholars, such as Mills (2003: 132), refer to Kendall and Wickham's method as "extremely irritating" yet "very useful (but very prescriptive)." Kendall and Wickham's method is composed of four cornerstones (history, Archaeology, Genealogy, and discourse), which are discussed in Chapter Three.

Overview of the Study

At present, no substantive equivalent exists within the arena of contemporary U.S. drug policy debate that might compare to the high levels of public awareness associated with the present topic of medicinal marijuana. As contemporary marijuana users are increasingly relabeled by successful state level drug policy ballot initiatives, large numbers are being redefined from criminals to patients. Currently, the debate over the legitimacy of medicinal marijuana use in America may very well accelerate.

A strict social constructionist position informs scholars that substances (such as marijuana) do not exist outside of their socially constructed definitions and meanings. By adopting the above position, marijuana is viewed here as a social construction; nothing more and nothing less. Marijuana was and is what social processes, such as criminalization and medicalization, construct it to be.

In the next chapter of the book, the analytical models used in the study are discussed. Here, medicalization theory, Foucaultian principles, as well as Currie's conceptual framework are connected. Then in Chapter Three, the study's methodology is discussed. Chapter Four examines the historical process of marijuana criminalization, illustrating the way by which the prohibition of marijuana occurs over the course of many decades. Finally, in Chapter Five, the second process of deviant designation change is examined. This chapter brings together the public policy implications medicalizing marijuana that are discussed throughout this research.

The overall aim of this study is to build upon Conrad and Schneider's medicalization theory by employing Kendall and Wickham's method. In an effort to understand how these two different processes of criminalization and medicalization are used by state and federal agencies, both processes are examined for their ability to regulate citizen behavior.

Chapter Two
The Three Stages of Deviant Designation

In this chapter, I connect elements of three different theories, each of which has a different level of analysis. The resulting three-stage theory connects some of the conceptual contributions made by Conrad and Schneider, Foucault and Currie. After connecting these micro, mid-range, and macro theoretical frameworks, I locate politically powerful claims-makers on various sides of the debate as they socially construct what people know about medical marijuana. My area of interest represents an opportunity to connect sociological and criminological theory and research to public policy, while also implicitly utilizing Kendall and Wickham's methodological approach. I also show how Foucault's five principles (Fillingham, 1993: 120-125) can bridge the conceptual and analytical gap between Conrad and Schneider's micro-level tenets and Currie's macro-level tenets.

Using Conrad and Schneider to Identify and Locate Deviant Designation Change

Conrad and Schneider's medicalization theory identifies five sequential steps in the process of medicalization. Before a conduct is criminalized or medicalized, it must first exist under the definition of deviant. Discoverers of immoral epidemics or medicinal applications, according to Conrad and Schneider, are analogous to miners looking for gold and staking claims. Thus, I can find Archaeological evidence of the existence of these miners (i.e., claims-makers and moral entrepreneurs) and the claims they have staked-out (i.e., initiated legislation). In this book, the process by which a social problem is initially identified, defined, and redefined is central to the inquiry. More specifically, both Conrad and Schneider

7

focus on the way by which individuals and special interest organizations initially construct, market, and actively perpetuate deviance designations.

The manner by which individuals and organizations seek and establish legitimacy for newly proposed deviance designations is also of import. Conflicts play out in courts and legislative bodies. Laws, court rulings, and legislative acts represent deeds of miners' conceptual, institutional, and interactional property. As miners come to own newly acquired property, the status of owner becomes semi-permanent. If codification of ownership into law occurs, the status becomes anchored, but never completely permanent. Deeds can always be unanchored by future challenges to the owners' conceptual, institutional, and interactional property (Conrad and Schneider, 1992).

Conrad and Schneider summarize their theory of medicalization in less than ten pages, in which they posit a two-part theory, each part containing five tenets. In a 1992 paper, Conrad clarifies what he means when discussing the process of medicalization. He states,

> The key to medicalization is the definitional use. Medicalization consists of defining a problem in medical terms, using medical language to describe a problem, adopting a medical framework to understand a problem, or using a medical intervention to "treat" it. This is a sociocultural process that may or may not involve the medical profession. Medicalization occurs when a medical frame or definition has been applied to understand or manage a problem; this is true for epilepsy as for "gender dysphoria" (transexualism). The interest in medicalization has predominately focused on previously nonmedical problems that have been medicalized (and, often, thought to be inappropriately medicalized), but actually medicalization must include all problems that come to be defined in medical terms (Conrad 1992: 211).

This definition describes the actual process of medicalization as well as the intrinsic impact which process can have on redefining a social problem.

The first part of Conrad and Schneider's two-part theory is composed of five tenets called, A Five Stage Sequential Model for the Medicalization of Deviance. The five stages are:

- Definition of Behavior as Deviant
- Prospecting: Medical Discovery
- Claims-Making: Medical and Nonmedical Interests
- Legitimacy: Securing Medical Turf
- Institutionalization of a Medical Deviance Designation

The first part of Conrad and Schneider's theory begins with the first tenet: Definition of Behavior as Deviant. Before a conduct or action receives a medical term or a medical definition, it must first exist under the definition of deviant. The first stage of the sequential model also contends that both labels of bad and sick are judgments of immorality (Conrad and Schneider, 1992: 266-7). The second tenet of the model is Prospecting: Medical Discovery. The second tenet contends that medical discoveries appearing in medical journals may compare to a miner (i.e., a medical researcher) prospecting for gold (i.e., new and/or different forms and uses for knowledge) and staking claims (i.e., publications involving the discoveries) on social space (i.e., conceptual, institutional, and/or interactional turf previously not held by the medical profession). Once a new diagnosis emerges from the professional literature, a new social problem is defined or redefined as a particular form of deviant behavior and may be brought into public view as belonging to the medical industrial complex (Conrad and Schneider, 1992: 266-7).

The third tenet in Conrad and Schneider's model, Claims Making: Medical and Nonmedical Interests, elucidates the process of construction for a new deviant designation. Here,

> . . . champions, moral entrepreneurs, and organized interests begin actively to make claims for a new deviance designation and attempt to expand the medical social control turf. Both medical and nonmedical interests engage in claims-making activities (Conrad and Schneider, 1992: 266-7).

The fourth tenet, Legitimacy: Securing Medical Turf describes the medical claims and their efforts to seek state legitimacy and official recognition. The conflict plays out in the official arenas of the courts and legislative bodies. Victory at this level for the medical claims-makers can result in issuing a deed to the industrial medical complex that establishes the newly acquired conceptual, institutional, and interactional property as the professional medical community owns it (Conrad and Schneider, 1992: 266-7). The last tenet of Conrad and Schneider's theory is the Institutionalization of a Medical Deviance Designation. Here, the new deviance designation is codified into law and institutionalized through new programming initiatives. The new definition is now legitimate and becomes semi-permanent, anchoring the new deviance designation against future challenges to its legitimacy and status quo privilege (Conrad and Schneider, 1992: 266-7).

The second part of Conrad and Schneider's theory is composed of five theoretical statements, "The Five Grounded Generalizations" (Conrad and Schneider, 1992: 165-74). These five generalizations are:

- Medicalization and demedicalization of deviance are cyclical phenomena.
- Medical designations of deviance are more often promoted as "foil" against criminal definitions than as ends in themselves.
- Only a small segment of the medical profession is involved in the medicalization of deviance.
- When medical designations of deviance are proposed, they most likely will be based on the notion of "compulsivity".
- Medicalization and demedicalization are political and not scientific achievements.

The first generalization of this second part posits that medicalization and demedicalization of deviance are cyclical phenomena. Conrad and Schneider contend that the designations of bad and sick move back and forth over time. They state, "We ought not be surprised at the fluidity between badness and sickness designations, this ebb and flow occurs in a common sea of 'immorality'" (Conrad and Schneider, 1992: 271). By defining the deviant as sick, Conrad and Schneider affirm, the judgment of immorality is kept. As a result, the extreme of either produces a climate that welcomes the counterclaims of the other (Conrad and Schneider, 1992: 271-2).

Conrad and Schneider's second generalization (that a medical designation of deviance can foil a criminal definition) ties into to the cyclical phenomena previously mentioned. Extreme criminalization of deviant behavior provides the fertile ground on which medicalization can emerge. Conversely, extreme medicalization of deviant behavior can provide the fertile conditions through which criminalization can emerge. Conrad and Schneider's third generalization asserts that only a small segment of the medical profession is involved in the medicalization of deviance. According to Conrad and Schneider, only a few physicians are themselves claims-makers. Most medical professionals are not familiar with cutting-edge debates and battles over the medicalization of deviant behaviors, which promote substantive societal change. Only after a new deviance definition is successfully designated (i.e., staked) within the parameters of newly acquired medical social-control turf, do rank and file physicians begin to deal with the problem behaviors or conditions associated with the new designation (Conrad and Schneider, 1992: 271-2).

The fourth generalization contends that when medical designations of deviance are proposed, they are based on the notion of compulsivity. Compulsivity refers to the way in which some actors (who habitually engage in deviant behavior) cannot resist the compulsion to engage repeatedly in deviant behavior and embrace the definition of powerless. In other words, once medicalized the deviant individuals are deviant not because of their own intents or moral failings.

The last assertion is Conrad and Schneider's most powerful. They posit that medicalization and demedicalization are political and not scientific achievements. While scientific-research often supports the arguments of medical claims-makers, scientific-research can also undermine those very arguments. Succeeding in the recognition and legitimization of claims is always a political achievement with close ties to capitalist interest. Contests are political and are not subject to the rules of an unbiased scientific method in pursuit of some sort of abstract absolute "truth". Together, Part I and Part II of medicalization theory represent a powerful theoretical tool for understanding how extreme criminalization can set the stage for the medicalization of certain deviant forms of behavior.

Building on Conrad and Schneider: Generalizing Medicalization Theory

Medicalization theory, in its current and orthodox form, would be incongruent with the method I am using. In order to better align medicalization theory with the method, I de-emphasize the causal logic associated with the sequential ordering of Conrad and Schneider's five stages.

I express the first four of Conrad and Schneider's five stages as structural contingencies associated with the successful emergence of a new deviant designation. Should all four of these contingencies be present within the same periods of time and geographical locations for extended periods, the new deviant designation is more likely to emerge and become institutionalized, officially recognized, as well as internalized by the populace. Conversely, should fewer than all four of these contingencies be present at different time periods or geographical locations for extended or brief periods, a new deviance designation is less likely to emerge and to successfully receive semi-permanent status. Here, the deviant designation is less likely to emerge through codification into criminal or administrative law.

As I generalize and frame medicalization theory in terms of contingencies instead of causalities, the slightly modified model is restated here as the Criminalization Model of Deviant Designation Change. For my purposes, the Criminalization Model is my diagnostic tool as I conceptualize the social history of marijuana as an arena where key players struggle for legitimacy and consensus. Within such an arena, both processes (criminalization and medicalization) are in contest for sovereignty. Through employing the Archaeology and Genealogy in

Chapters Four and Five, I describe each process and define the conflict between them both, while also ordering all of the evidentiary information. The actors of discourses (i.e., the players) interact cooperatively and competitively within the field (i.e., yesterday and today's history), but most importantly, their actions are contingent upon all of the other actions that are in play within the times and geographic confines of my historical analysis.

Figure 2.1 – Criminalization Model of Deviance Designation Change

Source: Adapted with modifications from Conrad and Schneider's (1992) Five Stage Sequential Model.

Figure 2.1 restates Part I of Conrad and Schneider's medicalization theory in non-sequential, contingent form. As my work builds upon medicalization theory, I intend to refrain from artificially privileging one contingency over another, either in order or in importance.

The first contingency of the slightly altered theory begins with the simple assertion, Definition of Behavior as Deviant. The next contingency, Prospecting: Discovery and Publicity, posits that discoveries in different media settings of criminal behaviors are comparable to the actions of miners. These miners compare to moral entrepreneurs prospecting for gold. Here, gold would be analogous to new and/or different uses for the correctional industrial complex. Within such a setting, these moral entrepreneurs stake claims and discover epidemics of immorality while they also push "tough on crime" policy initiatives. Here, a growing correctional industrial complex successfully seizes legal, institutional, and/or interactional turf previously not held by the law enforcement professions. Once a new law emerges from a legislative body and a new social problem or crime is born, the old behavior receives a new label of crime, and soon belongs to the correctional industrial complex (Conrad and Schneider, 1992: 266-267).

The next contingency, Claims Making: Values of Special Interest Groups examines the way by which new criminal designations are constructed and reinforced. Legislators, claims makers, moral entrepreneurs, bureaucratic oligarchy and special interest groups begin actively to make claims and lobby for a new criminalization designation. By these actions, they attempt to enlarge criminal justice social control turf via bureaucratic expansion, to secure budgetary priority, political influence, and increase authoritative moral prowess. Both legal and non-legal interests throughout the process engage in claims-making activities (Conrad and Schneider, 1992: 266-267).

Next, Conrad and Schneider's fourth contingency, Securing Professional Turf, describes the claims made by political actors and celebrity speakers seeking legitimacy and official recognition, not only for themselves as members of the associated oligarchy, but for the very institutions which might prosper under the proposed policy changes. Conflicts play out in the official arenas of the courts and legislative bodies but also emerge from long fought propaganda campaigns that influence citizens and resonate through media representations and counter representations. Here, written, visual and auditory forms of media proliferate and become accepted as "truth". The new truth brand snowballs into unquestioned fact. Victory at this level for the hard driving claims makers might result in an ownership deed for the correctional industrial complex. As a result, the professional criminal justice community owns the newly acquired conceptual, institutional, and interactional property. It is here that criminal justice practitioners take ownership of the newly designated crime (Conrad and Schneider, 1992: 266-267).

The last contingency I discuss, with respect to the Criminalization Model of Deviance Designation Change, is the Institutionalization of an Emergent (i.e., criminal) Deviance Designation. Here, the newly criminalized designation is codified into law and institutionalized through bureaucratization. The new definition is now legitimate and semipermanent, anchoring against future challenges to its legitimacy as a real criminal action (Conrad and Schneider, 1992: 266-267). For a more contemporary example, I use marijuana as it is presently classified by the federal government as a Schedule I substance (i.e., a drug with no medical value).

The Schedule I definition of marijuana continually moves the drug out of a medical sphere of authority and the criminalization of the drug at the federal level is sustained. Henceforth, its label of illegitimacy is always in production, regardless of the many different state level decriminalization/medicalization initiatives. Since federal law supersedes state law, even the legitimate use of state sanctioned medicinal marijuana continues to be illegal by the institutionalized total prohibition of the drug at the federal level. The result is the unending reproduction of the drug's present air of illegitimacy.

The second part of the Criminalization Model of Deviant Designation Change is composed of five theoretical statements that slightly modify Conrad and Schneider's earlier work. I refer to these new modified generalizations as The Five Grounded Generalizations for the Criminalization of Deviance. The second part of this two-part theory and its five subparts are as follows:

- Medicalization and criminalization of deviance are cyclical phenomena.
- Medical designations of deviance often "foil" official semipermanent criminal definitions. Likewise, criminal designations of deviance often "foil" official semipermanent medical definitions.
- Only a small segment of the medical profession is involved in the medicalization of deviance. Likewise, only a small segment of the criminal justice profession is involved in the criminalization of deviance.
- When medical designations of deviance are proposed, they most likely will be based on the notion of "compulsivity." When criminal designations are proposed, they most likely will be based on the existence of an "epidemic of immorality and lawlessness."
- Medicalization and criminalization are political and not scientific achievements.

The first generalization of the second part of the Criminalization Model of Deviance Designation Change asserts that the criminalization and medicalization of deviance are cyclical phenomena. Conrad and Schneider contend that the designations of bad and sick move back and forth over time. By defining the deviant as criminal, the judgment of immorality remains. The second generalization of the Criminalization Model asserts that criminal designations of deviance often foil official semi-permanent medical definitions. Extreme medicalization of deviant behavior can provide the conditions through which criminalization can emerge.

The third generalization asserts that only a small segment of the criminal justice profession is involved in the criminalization of deviance. Only a few members of the law enforcement community are claims makers themselves. Most criminal justice professionals are unaware of the cutting-edge debates and battles that promote substantive drug policy change. Only after a new deviance definition is successfully criminalized (i.e., designated or staked out) within the parameters of newly acquired criminal justice social-control turf, do the rank and file law enforcement practitioners begin to deal with the problem behaviors or conditions associated with the newly criminalized designation (Conrad and Schneider, 1992: 271-272).

The fourth generalization contends that when criminal designations of deviance are proposed, they are associated with the existence of epidemics of immorality and lawlessness. Epidemics of immorality and lawlessness refer to the way in which large numbers of societal actors (who routinely engage in deviant behavior) are not resisting the urge to engage repeatedly in the said deviant behaviors. The claims makers repeatedly assert these deviant individuals are deviant because of their own immoral actions and choices. The claims makers assert that deviants only refrain from their immoral and destructive behaviors if there are harsh legal consequences for their deviant (now criminal) actions.

The last assertion of the Criminalization Model of Deviance Designation Change is most emphatic in the way it posits criminalization as a process. Here, criminalization is a political (not scientific) achievement. Scientific research may support the arguments of anti-drug claims-makers or undermine the very same anti-drug assertions. Succeeding in the recognition and legitimization of claims is always a political achievement. Contests are political and not subjected to the rules of an unbiased scientific method in pursuit of some sort of abstract absolute truth. To summarize, my study posits that Part I and Part II of the recently christened Criminalization Model of Deviance Designation Change may represent a useful theoretical tool for understanding the way by which marijuana criminalization emerged within the specific period and geographic setting of the first half of the · twentieth century America.

Using Foucault to Clarify How a New Deviant Designation is Institutionalized

The second stage of my theoretical approach may be analogous to the means of new label production, or the five principles of Foucault's Science of Discipline. As programming incentives trickle down from policy makers to state and federal bureaucracies, institutional directives begin to operate on the public. These five principles attempt to illustrate the way by which citizens become submissive to governmental control and regulation. For instance, imagine that Foucault's five principles, which make up his Science of Discipline, are easily summarized in an illustration of five concentric circles. Each lesser tenet is contained or nested within a greater tenet.

Figure 2.2 – Fillingham's Five Principles of Foucault's Science of Discipline

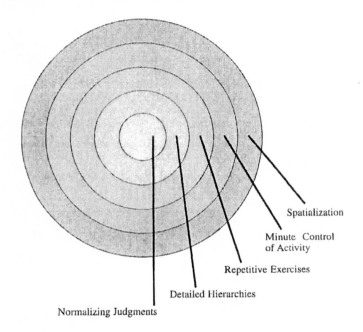

Source: Fillingham, 1993: 120-125.

The Principle of Spatialization

"Spatialization" occurs in prisons the same way that it occurs in universities or hospitals. Each citizen has specific places where he or she must be during specific times on specific days. These places indicate not only what the subject does, but also who the subject is. These times and places actually define the citizens as they are described through their willing or unwilling participation in the process of spatialization. Within this context, proper timing is just as critical as proper physical placement for the disciplined citizen undergoing behavioral modification. To meet the demands of spatialization, is to avoid the negative repercussions of being labeled abnormal/immoral/unknowledgeable and, ultimately, powerless.   Hence, the expression "being at the right place at the right time" takes on true significance within the life course of the citizen trying to navigate through the many different bureaucratic encounters that take place throughout the life course (Fillingham, 1993: 120-125).

The Minute Control of Activity

Citizens undergoing institutionalized discipline use timetables and schedules to regulate their activities within the framework of spatialization. Class schedules, itineraries, calendars, and multiple deadlines that require multitasking and punctuality are all examples of how even the most minute and remote activities of disciplined subjects are controlled. In a sense, the American experience itself relates to the way by which individuals navigate through bureaucracies and other large social institutions, charged with engineering or modifying the behavior of the citizens. Bureaucratic institutions may not operate according to their original design, but they do operate. Additionally, these institutions play an important role in an individual's placement within the social order. Especially in ritualism, institutional socialization gets its work done and is allied with and works through language. While some formal systems of discipline may have broken down, other new informal systems of discipline have flourished. Regardless of the systems' formal or informal apparatus of discipline, the process of discipline still exemplifies Foucault's model (Fillingham, 1993: 120-125).

The Principle of Repetitive Exercise

Through spatialization and the minute control of activity, citizens begin to internalize external prompts for action. Simply put, as citizens experience the impact of institutionalization, they begin to speak and act in institutionally sanctioned ways. Through repetitive exercises, subjects can learn to master institutionally preferred ways of thinking, acting, speaking and being (Fillingham, 1993: 120-125).

Detailed Hierarchical Structures

Within spatialization, the activities of citizens are the objects of control, down to the minutest of activities. Within the minute control of these activities, citizens routinely engage in activities that are repetitive in nature. Here, constant repetition (i.e. training or practice) breeds predicted automations to conditioning stimuli. The rate of progress made by the disciplined individual is the study of authority figures. Later, the individual, through standardization, enters into an assemblage of like-minded or physically able individuals (Fillingham, 1993: 120-125). As the disciplined repeat exercises, higher strata of authority observe the disciplined. Those in charge of the lower ranks are the subject of more training, and observation by higher levels of authority. These structural hierarchies are complex, detailed, and attached to one another, keeping watch over one another through formal and informal mechanisms of control and discipline. In burden, those doing the disciplining are also being disciplined.

Disciplinary power works on individuals internally and is administered externally in not only overt manners but in subtle ways, such as nonverbal communication, facial expressions of submission, and emotions emerging when praise is received and punishment is adverted (Fillingham, 1993: 125). When the administration of disciplinary power is thorough and efficient, disciplined individuals can even become emotionally attached to their supervisors, bonding much in the manner of a child with its parent(s). Lastly, it is important to restate that nearly all those meting out disciplinary power are also on the receiving end of disciplinary power (Fillingham, 1993: 120-125).

Judgment Normalization

According to Foucault's five principles, the benchmark by which authority figures judge newly disciplined citizens is their associate identity of normal or abnormal (Fillingham, 1993: 125). Fillingham (1993: 13) uses Foucault's five principles to show that all of the social sciences share the common ground of their central mechanism (i.e., the categorization of subjects into normal and abnormal). For example, education Ph.D.s might identify the learning disabled. Linguists might identify speech impediments. Doctors identify diseases within the ill. Psychiatrists identify different forms of mental illnesses (Fillingham, 1993: 13-18).

Whether or not these labels are empirically valid and reliable is not important. These labels of abnormality produce subject classifications of this or that, one or the other, us or them, law abiding or criminal, well or ill, etc. Over time, the statements of the claims makers become observable symptoms. The populace learns how to recognize these symptoms as visible manifestations of the truth inherent in the claims makers' message. For example, the populace can only identify a marijuana criminal or a marijuana patient once they receive instruction from the claims makers in what specifically to look for and identify accordingly. The morality or lack thereof with respect to any labeling procedure is inconsequential. What is of importance is how the label of abnormal carries with it other labels of association. The label of abnormal carries with it the stigma of immoral, bad, or criminal. In illustrating, Fillingham (1993: 8-9) indirectly speaks of criminologists and criminology:

> When we're talking about knowledge of human beings, the social sciences, or, as Foucault calls them, 'the human sciences,' then the people deciding what is true (constructing Truth) are deciding matters that define humanity, and affect people in general. If they can get enough people to believe what they have decided, then that may be more important than some unknowable truth. . . How do some people get the rest of us to accept their ideas of who we are? That involves

some power to create belief. And these same people who decide what is knowledge in the first place can easily claim to be the most knowledgeable . . . to know more about us than we do ourselves.

Thus, the criminologist may be mistaken to find comfort in the notion that no one is paying attention to the public policy implications of his or her work. While it may be correct to assume that while no one is listening, no harm takes place; the unintended implications of academic work may, in fact, have a greater impact on fellow citizens than the researcher may have initially imagined.

Using Currie to Account for the Overproduction of Deviant Designations

The last stage of my theoretical framework is associated with the structural conditions under which the exponential production of a newly created and institutionalized deviant designation can occur. While Conrad and Schneider describe how new deviant designations originate and Foucault specifies the way by which labeling is implemented and institutionalized, Elliot Currie (1968: 351) describes how criminal designations can sometimes undergo mass reproduction and proliferate into a machine for the production of deviants (Currie 1968: 351). Here, I attempt to illustrate what Currie's "enormously effective machine" actually is, as well as how Currie's ideas can connect to the theoretical tenets of the science of discipline and the model of criminalization.

Currie laid out his approach in a 1968 paper entitled, "Crimes without Criminals: Witchcraft and Its Control in Renaissance Europe." In the article, Currie puts forth a conceptual framework that is helpful to the present investigation. He identifies three characteristics that enabled the continental [European] legal order to be "an enormously effective machine for the systematic and massive production of confessed deviants [witches]" (Currie 1968: 351-352). According to Currie, the three main characteristics of this legal order are as follows:

- A high degree of structured interest in the apprehension and processing of deviants.

- Systematic establishment of extraordinary powers for suppressing deviance, with a concomitant lack of internal restraints.
- Invulnerability to restraint from other social institutions.

Currie focuses on particular type of control structure that might result in extremely high rates of deviance. He describes a system of repressive control that bears a striking resemblance to the history of marijuana prohibition in America. I reframe the above characteristics as four separate characteristics within the present investigation. In restating Currie's characteristics, I intend to demonstrate the relevance of Currie's assertions within the context of contemporary inquiries into American history.

In keeping with Kendall and Wickham's methodological device, I recast Currie's characteristics of deviant production as contingencies, deemphasizing any implicit sequential ordering and/or causal implication. The present study restates Currie's characteristics as follows:

- A high degree of structured interest in the apprehension and processing of deviants.
- Systematic establishment of extraordinary powers for suppressing deviance.
- A concomitant lack of internal restraints.
- Invulnerability to restraint from other social institutions.

Currie's four characteristics are not restricted to any specific time or place in history. While the specific target of his original inquiry was the social control of witchcraft in Continental Europe during the Renaissance, his four characteristics are flexible and translate well within the context of my historical analysis.

High Degree of Structured Interest: Apprehending and Processing Newly Designated Deviants

According to Currie, one of the most significant characteristics of "an enormously effective machine" for the production of deviants is a court system's authority to confiscate the properties and or assets and accuse subjects of practicing officially prohibited behavior. Confession is not always required to provide the courts with a powerful motive for the mass stigmatization of subjects newly labeled as criminal. Large-scale industries sustain and create more deviants via the accusation of more deviants and the confiscation of their privately owned property (Currie 1968: 356). For a contemporary illustration I quote, *Our Right to Drugs*, by Thomas Szasz (1992: 22) below:

> One of the most ominous and least publicized consequences of the War on Drugs is the government's use of the Internal Revenue Service and of the international banking system to detect and apprehend persons engaged in the drug trade, along with its practice of confiscating property from persons accused of drug offences even when they are innocent. These measures illustrate that the War on Drugs is, literally, a war on property – waged by the U.S. government with the enthusiastic support of the Supreme Court.

Currie encourages scholars to ask, who benefits? Frederic Bastiat may have answered the question best over a century and half ago when he retorted,

> The government offers to cure all the ills of mankind . . . . All that is needed is to create some new government agencies and to pay a few more bureaucrats. In a word, the tactic consists in initiating, in the guise of actual services, what are nothing but restrictions; thereafter, the nation pays, not for being served, but for being disserved. (Szasz, 1992: 95).

Systematic Establishment of Extraordinary Powers for Suppressing Deviance

Currie (1968: 346) asserts another significant characteristic of "an enormously effective machine" engineered and developed for the production of deviants and the empowerment of official agents of morally sanction causes. These agents employ the full force of the law to prosecute those who possess the new criminal designation, whatever it might be. Large numbers of prosecutions and convictions affirm the reality of the newly criminalized behavior as a serious social problem that requires official legal recognition, intervention and action. A contemporary example might be the way in which institutions of the American media or press might intensely focus on a particular social problem, which might temporarily possess a tremendous amount of political appeal. The attention given to the social problem of concern may in turn result in a collective sense of outrage held by the citizens informed by the media sources. National tragedies are often catalysts for change as they inherently contain tremendous political appeal.

Concomitant Lack of Internal Restraints

The concomitant lack of internal restraints is another characteristic identified by Currie. As newly empowered institutions and agents of social control begin to impose harsh penalties against even low-level participants of the prohibited activity, officials actively ignore the high fiscal and moral price of excessive punishment. Powerful institutions and actors charged with overseeing or checking abuses within accelerated systems of deviant behavior control fail in their duty to impose internal forms of restraint. In the words of journalist Eric Sevareid, "The chief cause of problems is solutions" (Duke and Gross 1993: 1).

Invulnerability to Restraint from Other Social Institutions

Disempowerment and structural exclusion often characterize newly labeled deviants. Newly criminalized citizens (i.e. criminals) become specific targets of massive social control initiatives. At times, unaccountability to other external sources of legitimate power and authority unfetter some of these social control initiatives. Sometimes, even contemporary and rationalized bureaucracies may engage in the active pursuit of commonplace deviants or harmless nonconformists. The collective hysteria may then result in increasing numbers of unintended casualties. As a result, the populace is encouraged to view unjustly treated citizens as collateral damage. The populace may then view the wrongly labeled as unfortunate isolated exceptions, justified as the unfortunate cost of doing business.

In an overzealous attempt to pursue those ceremoniously labeled deviant, any considerable challenge to any legal system interested in hunting down and suppressing these activities becomes a target for elimination or considerable relaxation (Currie, 1968: 347). Even the use of regular and systematic torture, by even the most civilized of social moral orders, may surface at the peak of collective panic. At times, the invented and perceived threat is so intense as to relax standards for witnesses within the courtroom and circumvent procedural safeguards (Currie 1968: 350).

Chapter Three
Kendall and Wickham's Method

Kendall and Wickham's method instructs researchers to view history as an action and not simply as an existing record of unquestionable interpretations of the past. By encouraging researchers to view historical research as something other than the examination of static records of unquestionable past interpretations, Kendall and Wickham's method guide researchers not in what to look for, but in how to look. In this manner, Kendall and Wickham assert that researchers can create a better investigation of their object of inquiry. Should researchers follow the methodological prescriptions below, Kendall and Wickham advise researchers to prepare themselves for surprising results.

This book adopts Galvin Kendall and Gary Wickham's manuscript, *Using Foucault's Methods,* because of its prescriptive approach to historical analysis. The method is composed of four separate "cornerstones", or themes, and each cornerstone is composed of a separate set of criteria for researchers to satisfy (Kendall and Wickham, 2000: 1). The four cornerstones are history[1], Archaeology, Genealogy[2], and discourse. In the discussion below, I summarize point-by-point, Kendall and Wickham's Foucaultian method in an accessible manner.

According to Kendall and Wickham, their method of qualitative analysis can assist researchers interested in examining a massive amount of historical and contemporary documentation. These authors also assert that the method assists researchers in systematically collecting, distilling, or condensing statements and

---

[1] Kendall and Wickham (2000: 22-3) define the action of "history" as "the exercise of cerebral and methodological hygiene by the researcher within the context of investigating, observing, diagnosing and reporting on the sum of thoughts and appearances with respect to a particular past and present problem of interest."
[2] Foucault refers to Genealogy as the "ontology of ourselves" or as exploring "the contemporary limits of the necessary" (Foucault, 1988: 95 and 1984:43).

documentation (i.e., data) that meets certain and specific criteria. I explain the specific criteria associated with each of the four cornerstones below. All data are eligible to pass through these four cornerstones, and the respective criteria associated with each cornerstone.

The Method's First Cornerstone: Historical Analysis

Within this cornerstone of the method, researchers must satisfy specific criteria to exercise proper "cerebral and methodological hygiene" as they investigate, observe, diagnose and report upon their problem of inquiry (Kendall and Wickham, 2000: 22-3). For researchers to employ Kendall and Wickham's method and conduct a history, researchers must: 1) "problematise" history, 2) spot contingencies, 3) be skeptical of all political arguments, and 4) suspend second order judgments. I define all four of these criteria below.

Problematise History

The first criterion that researchers are required to satisfy is to problematise history.[3] By asking researchers to problematise history, the method encourages scholars to reexamine and reinterpret historical documentation. "Problematising" history is a technique to illuminate interesting and neglected points of attention associated with researchers' areas of inquiry (Kendall and Wickham, 2000: 4). While the technique of "problematisation" means to disrupt existing interpretations of history (Kendall and Wickham, 2000: 4), the term "problematisation" also means that researchers must begin by specifying a problem to investigate, not a historical period.

Researchers should not select a historical time-period to investigate, but a problem to drive the investigation. It is critical that observers allow for the possibility of surprise as they reinterpret historical events through the examination of statements. In that way, the method encourages the "generation of surprising stories" (Kendall and Wickham, 2000: 22). The unusual character of "surprise" is

---

[3] For a researcher to "problematise" history, a researcher must seek to reinterpret history by rejecting existing interpretations of historical statements and documentation.

contained within the new analysis brought into being by using the technique of problematisation (Kendall and Wickham, 2000: 22). In this manner, researchers/ observers attempt to meet with the ultimate goal of the method, to generate an improved examination of the problem of interest (Kendall and Wickham, 2000: 23). Within the context of my research, the objects or problems of interest are the historical processes of marijuana criminalization and marijuana medicalization.

Spot Contingencies (Not Causes)

The second criterion that researchers are required to satisfy requires them to "spot contingencies" as a technique to analyze past and present statements, because they argue, historical situations contain countless contingencies (Kendall and Wickham, 2000: 5-9).[4] The emergence of any historical event is never imminent or necessary; all historical events depend on a number of miscellaneous relationships between other contingent events. That is, the method suggests breaking the habit of interpreting historical events as the result (or effect) of causal forces.

The method requires researchers to assume that no order is inherently present. Herein, these authors assert, researchers experience the value of "contingency spotting" (or the act of looking for contingencies), for contingency spotting can assist researchers in becoming less biased (Kendall and Wickham, 2000: 7-8). However, the method acknowledges that it is impossible for researchers to become completely unbiased and relativistic. What is of utmost importance is for researchers to continually attempt to become less biased. It is the attempt, which is of importance (Kendall and Wickham, 2000: 7-8).

Be Skeptical of All Political Arguments

The third criterion that researchers are required to satisfy is to distinguish between the helpfulness of skepticism and the damage associated with active cynicism. Skepticism encourages a vigilant, purposeful deferment of judgment on the part of observers, as statements undergo examination and reinterpretation. Cynicism is sarcastic and pessimistic, entailing negative viewpoints before any

---

[4] Contingencies are historical circumstances devoid of causal assumptions.

statement is subject to examination. Encouraging skepticism as a powerful method for attempting to suspend judgments as observers examine statements associated with past and present histories (Kendall and Wickham, 2000: 9-10), the method also instructs researchers to continually attempt to suspend judgment.

Researchers attempt to suspend judgments by setting out oppositions or by creating what Foucault referred to in *The History of Sexuality* (1978: 85) as a "binary system." A binary system is a way by which researchers may begin to view a statement or a thing as having two opposing conditions (i.e., black and white, good and bad, male and female). In *The History of Sexuality* (1978: 85) Foucault asserts, "Power is essentially what dictates its law to sex. Which means first of all that sex is placed by power in a binary system: licit and illicit, permitted and forbidden." Therefore, researchers must attempt to conceive oppositions by dividing all statements encountered into binary opposites. For example, if "Power is essentially what dictates its law to [marijuana, then marijuana] is placed by power in a binary system: licit and illicit, permitted and forbidden" (Foucault, 1978: 85). For researchers studying statements about marijuana, a continual attempt to create binary systems of thought tries to avoid utilizing notions of progress or regress. For researchers, the past is to be just as bizarre (or banal) as the present. Like the past, the present becomes less desirable and less sensible and political arguments become increasingly suspect (Kendall and Wickham, 2000: 4).

Suspending Second-Order Judgments

According to Kendall and Wickham (2000: 13), historical observation is sometimes used as a vehicle to forward the assumption that the future holds potential for progress even when the present holds no such evidence of progress existing. When researchers view and subsequently judge the past worse than the present, Kendall and Wickham (2000: 13) refer to these assumptions as "the liberal error." Conversely, observers of past and present social phenomena who assume that the past was somehow a qualitatively better period are committing what Kendall and Wickham (2000: 13) refer to as "the Marxist error." To combat these problematic assumptions, the method recommends that researchers engage in the suspension of "second order judgments" (Kendall and Wickham, 2000: 11-14). Kendall and Wickham (2000: 15) illustrate how vulnerable observers of histories can be to influence from second-order judgments.

> Second order judgments tend to sneak in hiding under cloak of a mysterious figure being brought to bear on the object being analyzed. This 'mysterious figure' is usually a representative of the reading habit pointed to above, perhaps best identified by the name of a particular author, though this can be somewhat misleading. We suggest that the 'mysterious figure' who imports second order judgments into (many observers') accounts is Karl Marx. We suggest further that Marx is the culprit for much second order judging in the second half of the twentieth century (Kendall and Wickham, 2000: 15).

Nevertheless, the method does not go so far as to accuse researchers of being closet moral crusaders.

The method emphasizes the importance of the attempt (not the complete success of, but the attempt) to suspend judgments of the second order. Researchers must understand that they can never completely succeed in dispensing with all political claims (Kendall and Wickham, 2000: 17-8). Kendall and Wickham (2000: 19) contend, "Second order judgments lead straight to the search for hidden meanings." Looking for hidden meanings and the quest for the discovery of hidden meanings through disciplined, long-suffering, hard arduous work and intellectual prowess can result in an artificial value judgment entering into researchers' observations.

The Method's Second Cornerstone: Archaeological Analysis

Archaeology, according to Foucault (1972: 79), "describes discourses[5] as practices[6] specified in the element of the archive."[7] Below, Kendall and Wickham help to illuminate Foucault's brief definition of the Archaeology, because it is one of Foucault's most important analytical investigative devices.

> Archaeology helps us to explore the networks of what is said, and what can be seen in a set of social arrangements: in the conduct of an Archaeology, one finds out something about the visible in 'opening up' statements and something about the statement in 'opening up visibilities' (Kendall and Wickham, 2000: 25).

When Kendall and Wickham (2000: 24) define the cornerstone of Archaeology, they introduce more awkward terms such as "networks" and "visibilities." They even instruct researchers to engage in an unusual sounding task (e.g., "open up visibilities"). By exploring "the networks of what is said," Kendall and Wickham (2000: 24) are simply referring to the act of investigating the different frameworks, which order the statements that are associated with different discourses. For example, if statements are analogous to cans of food in a pantry then the shelves that the cans rest upon are "the networks of what is said." The "networks" are frameworks that serve to order the statements (e.g., canned meats are on the bottom shelves and canned vegetables are on the top selves).

It is important to emphasize that statements, for researchers using Kendall and Wickham's method, are the units of analysis. Therefore, when Kendall and Wickham (2000: 24) refer to the "opening up" of statements, they are simply saying that statements are going to be scrutinized, as they are found within "the archive" (i.e., the metaphoric pantry that contains all of the canned goods). In summation,

---

[5] For now, try to think of a "discourse" as a "system of thought" that is productive.

[6] Next, try to think of a "discourse" as a "practice" (i.e., as a process) that carries out a productive aim. By "productive aim," I mean the intended products of a system of thought. For another illustration, if the products of a discourse are the "goals" then the discourse is the "means."

[7] The researcher should not conceptualize "the archive" as a physical set of annals or collection of hard copy/original documents but rather as a conceptual and general representation of how testimonials are fashioned, conveyed, and reproduced (Kendall and Wickham, 2000: 24).

when Kendall and Wickham say something like, the "Archaeology is the process of investigating the archives of discourse" (Kendall and Wickham, 2000: 25), they simply mean that researchers conducting an Archaeology are engaging a particular investigative process, whereby a specific collection of historical documentation (i.e., the cans within the pantry) are identified, examined and described in a specific and systematic manner.

Kendall and Wickham argue that researchers conducting Archaeologies must describe: 1) statements in the archive that cover the visible and "sayable,"[8] 2) regularities of statements, 3) relations between one statement and other statements, 4) the formulation for the rules for the repeatability or use of statements, 5) positions which are established between subjects, 6) surfaces[9] of emergence, 7) institutions which acquire authority and provide limits, and 8) forms of speculation (Kendall and Wickham, 2000: 24-8).

Describing Statements in the Archive that Cover the Visible and "Sayable"

An Archaeological analysis of the criminalization of marijuana would first attempt to examine the "sayable" (i.e., statements utilizing words) with the visible (i.e., statements utilizing images) and vice versa (Kendall and Wickham, 2000: 27). For example, researchers/observers might want to concentrate on the gateway theory, as part of the "sayable" along with images (i.e., parading children in DARE t-shirts) as part of the visible.[10] Once again, words and things can sometimes mutually condition one another in a snowballing of images and expressions.

In addition, this first criterion of the Archaeology entails the timetabling of sets of statements and arrangements. By this means, the construction of new prisons, police stations, court building, treatment facilities, governmental offices (i.e., the visible) may be noted along with the emergence of laws, policies, advertising campaigns, media exposure, and educational programs (i.e., the "sayable"). For an

---

[8] The unusual terms, such as "the visible" and "the sayable," receive explanation below.

[9] Again, unusual terms, such as "surfaces," receive explanation below.

[10] In general, the gateway theory asserts that when individuals use marijuana they will eventually start using harder drugs and become a "drug addict." The theory asserts that marijuana use serves as a "gateway" to harder drugs and to addictive behavior.

example, researchers conducting an Archaeological analysis on the social history of marijuana might watch the film, *Reefer Madness*. In America's not so distant past, this film was a visibility that may have created statements about those who were bringing the recreational use of marijuana into play. In turn, this visibility (or film) and these statements (produced by people watching the film) may have produced new/additional and abundant forms of visibilities (i.e., newspaper reports, and magazine articles) about the drug itself and those who were using marijuana recreationally. These new "visibilities" ultimately may have produced more statements about the antisocial aspects of marijuana use.[11] In this way, researchers seek to describe statements that condition visibilities, as well as visibilities that may condition statements (Kendall and Wickham, 2000: 25).

Regularities of Statements in Non-Interpretive Manner

Kendall and Wickham encourage researchers to conduct Archaeological analyses, describing statement consistencies, discrepancies, mutations, and transformations. Researchers should attempt to circumvent judgmental evaluations of statements by not actively searching for authors, allowing statements and visibilities to become the focal point of the search. For those conducting an Archaeology, describing the surface meaning of the statement is important, not the search for concealed implications and conspiracies of action (Kendall and Wickham, 2000: 26).

Relations between One Statement and Other Statements

The method emphasizes that statements trickle down from orderly systems of communication that represent a hierarchical authority structure. Researchers are to assume that statements relate to each other via a downward flow of power (e.g., from the Office of National Drug Control Policy (ONDCP) to Drug Abuse Resistance Education (D.A.R.E.) officers to eleven-year-old children found within the states' public schooling apparatus). In summation, illustrating how a "system of

---

[11] The investigation looks at these historical statements and their emergence, not in the validity or legitimacy of these statements. It matters not that the claims made by those who created the now classic *Reefer Madness* film were false or true; what is of concern is the explicit temporal and spatial locations of these visibilities and statements (Kendall and Wickham, 2000: 25).

statements" operates in practice and appearance is important in creating the Archaeology (Kendall and Wickham, 2000: 27).

The Formulation of Rules for the Repeatability or Use of Statements

Kendall and Wickham require researchers to describe the rules for the repeatability of statements and the hierarchical channels that trickle power and knowledge downward to increasingly disciplined ranks of subjects. As a result, researchers must construct rules associated with statement repeatability (Kendall and Wickham, 2000: 27). Statements that systematically undergo repetition are more likely to become an accepted truth brand. For a more specific example of how these rules may form, I discuss a newspaper article that I came across while I was in Carthage, Missouri several years ago. At that time, I picked up a local paper called *The Carthage Press* because a front-page article caught my eye. The article was entitled "D.A.R.E. graduates vow to be drug free: 'WE CAN BE STRONG TOGETHER.'" In the photo that accompanied the article, a law enforcement agent was placing medals over the heads of the children who participated in a local elementary school D.A.R.E. graduation.

The article described the activities of young D.A.R.E. participants who wrote essays and performed in a D.A.R.E. choir. The choir is of interest because, for a child to learn a song in choir, the elementary school student must practice over and over the words and the music. "Sufficient repetition creates automatic reactions to stimuli" (Fillingham, 1993: 123). A choir can be an extremely useful method of instilling ideas into the minds of young subjects because the specific statements are repeated until the statements are committed to memory. They practice these statements/songs until it is time to perform in front of their parents, teachers, and larger community. By repeatedly announcing their allegiance to the established moral order, they commit to living by the D.A.R.E. dictum of illicit drug abstinence. Their repetitive voices, however, are not the only instruments by which the statements of D.A.R.E. enter into distribution.

The elementary students, on the front page of the paper, were receiving medals with red, white and blue ribbons around their necks. They had won the D.A.R.E. essay competition and received public acknowledgement for the "milestone" of graduating from the "Drug Abuse Resistance Education" program funded by federal and state tax dollars. The newspaper article is not clear on whether the celebration was for honoring sixth or eight graders. Nevertheless, the celebration appeared to be an officially recognized state sanctioned rite of passage, performed repeatedly each year.

The D.A.R.E. officer also taught other courses at the elementary school. He taught a first grade class about safety, a "Vega" class in fifth grade, and D.A.R.E. classes in sixth and eighth grades, whereby, students were writing essays. Before graduating, students had received repeated exposure to the D.A.R.E. program in different formats in different grades. The students' essays about drugs were of interest; a portion of the article is as follows:

> Students complete a workbook, commit to being drug free, and write an essay about the course. The essays give students a chance to write down their feelings in a medium that is not right or wrong. That's where the real, unscripted honesty comes out. Students confess to not realizing the dangers of drugs, the harm they can do, or the accessibility to them. [One D.A.R.E. student] wrote, "I've learned to get out of a situation without being hurt. I didn't realize what a bad world it is out there." (Putnam, 2004: 1A).

The quote reveals several points of interest. First, the environment in which the child is writing the essay is, by definition, neither "right nor wrong."

Before their introduction to D.A.R.E. programs, children are usually unaware of the state's stance on illicit substance use. They are also usually unaware of official state myths/facts about illicit substances. Next, the students "confess" (an interesting choice of wording) to not realizing the dangers of experimenting with illicit substances. State agents assess the children's ability to internalize these myths/facts by reading (i.e., repeating) the children's confessions, in essay format, in an environment that is neither "right nor wrong." The act of repeating their statements (i.e., essays) and proclaiming the validity of these statements as neither right nor wrong allows the statements of the children to receive the labels of unbiased or factual. The newly internalized information (i.e., drug war myths/facts) is then privileged into the real, through repetition, as truthful, unbiased, and as a matter of fact, not a matter of morality, judgment, or ideology.

Positions Established Between Subjects

By examining a statement and its capacity to repeat, the Archaeology also allows for the analysis of the positions between subjects (i.e., disciplined individuals) as they relate to the statements that might produce these positions. In the words of Kendall and Wickham (2000: 27), "Statements produce subject positions." Accordingly, subjects might begin to internalize specific ways of acting into specific states of being. These states of an individual's being are either congruent or incongruent with statements that he or she is required to make, within spatial and temporal positions. Such statements become legitimate through a hierarchical structure of power. As statements repeat overtime, they become part of the true, part of the real (Kendall and Wickham, 2000: 26-27).

Surfaces of Emergence

According to Kendall and Wickham, a "surface" is a place in which a subject (or citizen) is disciplined. Surfaces are places or institutions (e.g., prisons, factories, schools, hospitals, psyche wards, colleges, or government bureaucracies) that are in charge of the officially sanctioned, appropriate, and proper development of citizens/subjects. The programming strategy deemed appropriate for each specific place is the "domain" (Kendall and Wickham, 2000: 26-27).

The "domain" is the program designed to maximize the production and subsequent discipline of the subjects allocated to legitimately exist within a specific space at a specific time. For example, the boot camp method of socialization/ discipline may be appropriate for the armed forces to engineer the behavior of newly recruited warriors during wartime. However, the boot camp method is ineffective for teaching elementary school children how to read, write, and play peacefully with one another. Within the places of public education, the domain may be D.A.R.E. education program or an evidence-based violence prevention program.

Domains impact subjects whether they are adults or children, poor or rich, educated or uneducated, male or female. Each domain is set up so that the subjects can receive individualized as well as standardized training. People are the raw material upon which the domains act (Kendall and Wickham, 2000: 27). For another example, substance abuse treatment facilities may use a twelve-step program as their domain within the confines of inpatient treatment and behavior modification systems (i.e., a lock down psychiatric ward within a hospital). Authorities, in charge of institutions, introduce programming strategies that affect the behavior of the subjects. For example, children that graduate from a fifth grade D.A.R.E. program (i.e., anti-drug domain) should ideally be less likely to try an illicit substance than those children that did not participate in the D.A.R.E. program. Together, the surface (or place) and the domain or program represent a regimented form of coercion, disciplining the people of the state.

Institutions that Acquire Authority and Provide Limits

Kendall and Wickham also require researchers, utilizing the Archaeology, to describe how institutions acquire and reproduce authority. These institutions are responsible for imparting limitations (or providing limits) on the behavior of the people that the institution serves. For example, the violation of administrative or criminal law may bring attention to the subject, as someone doing something unacceptable, and the subject may then become the object of disciplinary action. As a result, the institution must "provide limits" to the transgressor (i.e., punish him/her).

Institutions are places of visibility (e.g., prisons), in which spatial arrangements (e.g., cellblocks) contribute to the programming of citizens/subjects for more acceptable forms of behavior (Kendall and Wickham, 2000: 28). To illustrate the way by which institutions acquire authority and provide limits to the behaviors of those that interact with these institutions, I discuss some major trends that took place during the past two decades. For example, in 1982, the Reagan administration spent $1.65 billion on the drug war. In 1998, the Clinton administration requested $17.1 billion for its drug war bureaucracies (Shelden and Brown, 2003: 385-386). These increases in budgetary priority allowed for the construction of new prisons, police stations, court buildings, governmental offices (i.e., institutions of the visible) throughout the 1980s and 1990s. Along with these changes, more anti-drug laws, policies, advertising campaigns, media exposure, and educational programs (i.e., institutions of the "sayable") emerged. During these two decades, even low-level marijuana use became less normal. In the words of William Bennett, America's first officially recognized drug czar:

> The fundamental mistake we made in the '70s is we said 'The user is not a problem. The user's the victim. We just have to get the dealer and the kingpin. Forget about the user.' The user then felt morally off the hook- not culpable, not responsible. 'It's the big boys in South America and the middle-sized boys in the big cities, but not me.' The casual user, the weekend user, the so-called recreational user- that person needs to be confronted and face consequences, too. We need to put laws in place (Bergman, L., Levis, K., Hamilton, D., and Zill, O., 2000).

Bennett's public campaign took place during the 1980s. His intent was to frame casual drug using behavior as not normal or even socially unacceptable. Bennett called the approach "denormalization" and behaviors that were once normal in the 1970s, were not normal and even criminal in the 1980s.

Bennett once said, "User accountability laws must establish that involvement in the illegal drug trade has clear consequences" (Bergman, Levis, Hamilton, and Zill, 2000). However, some the consequences associated with the passage of some of the "user accountability laws" of the 1980s was the growth of America's correctional industrial complex as well as the number of individuals incarcerated within such a system. In summation, institutions that acquire authority can introduce and provide new limits of behavior. Over time, these institutions may acquire more authority in the attempt to regulate the behavior (i.e., provide limits) of more individuals.

Forms of Specification

The eighth criterion that researchers are required to satisfy asks them to describe how discursively produced subjects (e.g., "drug addicts") become targets for systematic applications of disciplinary action (e.g., arrest and incarceration). By focusing on discursively produced subjects (e.g., PhDs, MDs, ex-cons, alcoholics, or drug addicts), researchers can attempt to make the historical process associated with discursively produced statements (i.e., "I need a fix.") and discursively produced visibilities (i.e., "That guy looks like a junkie.") accessible for scrutiny. For another example, the discourse associated with substance-abuse outpatient treatment (e.g., AA or NA groups) encourages subjects to hold on to a specific set of definitions. These definitions (or complex of thoughts) connect the alcohol or drug "addict" to all of the "recovering addicts" who eagerly engage in the learning, speaking, and teaching the AA and/or NA discourses to the newest "addict" member of the group. The "recovering addicts," introduce the newest members to the AA and/or NA discourses (or complex of definitions) that serve to connect all members to one another. The very discourses that require their committed participation produce "addicts" and "recovering addicts." In this way, people receive different labels, or different "forms of specification."

The Method's Third Cornerstone: Genealogical Analysis

Foucault once said, "Let us give the term 'Genealogy' to the union of erudite knowledge and local memories which allows us to establish a historical knowledge of struggles and to make use of this knowledge tactically today" (Foucault, 1977: 42). By "erudite knowledge," Foucault was referring to the mainstreamed complexes of information that overshadow less popular voices of history. By "local memories," Foucault alludes to ordinary viewpoints and perceptions of the here and now. To define Genealogy is to fuse these two types of information and understanding (erudite and local) into one system of delivery that highlights these past and present "less popular" voices of history – to popularize the unpopular with a novel voice.

Kendall and Wickham (2000: 28) define Genealogy, the third cornerstone, as "a methodological weapon used to reinterpret established, rested and/or entrenched forms of intellectual analysis by opening up their origins and functions for skeptical scrutiny." For these two authors (2000: 34), researchers should use a Genealogy to describe today's history in six separate ways. More specifically, researchers that conduct a Genealogy must describe: 1) and analyze disreputable origins and unpalatable functions, 2) power through the history of the present, 3) and make uncomfortable existing analyses, 4) statements as motion pictures or as an ongoing practice, 5) the web of discourse, and 6) problems of the present while emphasizing power.

A Genealogy Describes and Analyzes Disreputable Origins and Unpalatable Functions

To conduct a Genealogy, Kendall and Wickham (2000: 29) assert that researchers must describe and analyze the conditions and consequences associated with their research problems. For example, researchers examining the contemporary marijuana medicalization movement should question the consequences of medicalizing marijuana. At the same time, researchers should intentionally be as unbiased as possible (Kendall and Wickham, 2000: 29). Researchers should not assume that the origins of thought associated with medicalizing marijuana are trustworthy or untrustworthy, agreeable or not agreeable, palatable or unpalatable, reputable or disreputable.

A Genealogy Describes Power through the History of the Present

While both Archaeology and Genealogy involve the "examination of bodies of statements with the archive," the Genealogy is an emergent inquiry into the "history of the present" (Kendall and Wickham, 2000: 29). For example, a Genealogy of today's American drug war may question the legitimacy, outcomes, and functions of contemporary prohibition. The Genealogy attempts to remove the fog of the present through describing contemporary relationships of power within the context of present historical events.

A Genealogy Describes and Makes Uncomfortable Existing Analyses

Ultimately, a Genealogy may allow participants within systems of thoughts to understand their own involvement in devising intellectual communities and perpetuating ideas (Kendall and Wickham, 2000: 30). In other words, even those who create empirical truth brands or empirical realities (i.e., researchers conducting scientific analysis) may begin to view their own participation within their own social environment more reflexively. In short, researchers conducting a Genealogy are required to reinterpret existing analyses and question the established and approved knowledge base.

Statements as Motion Pictures or as an Ongoing Practice

Genealogy and Archaeology are distinguishable from one another by the way these methodological devices approach the fourth principle of the method: discourse. Metaphorically, an Archaeological analysis attends to the photographs of a family album that, in total, make up the object of study.[12] The proverbial family album may be fragmented, but it is historically horizontal. Archaeology attends to the "processual" past. Genealogy is specifically oriented to study the "processual" present and its continuous disposition. Genealogy would be akin to a short home movie of the family's most recent important event (Kendall and Wickham, 2000: 30). The family's metaphoric home movie may be short, but it is continuous, relevant and historically vertical. Genealogy is simply the application of Archaeology as a methodological apparatus to lay bare the discourse of the here and now.

The Web of Discourse

Subjects (i.e., human beings) subjugated to discursive reign are the least likely to be privy to the totalizing influence of its impulses and conditions.

---

[12] Once again and for now, try to think of a discourse as a system of thought or a complex of knowledge. The Genealogy of this book targets the discourse associated with medicalizing marijuana. The Archaeology of this book targets the discourse associated with criminalizing marijuana.

Genealogy is a strategy for allowing observers to use the method of the Archaeology to break from the totalizing influence of the discursive web that all citizens are subject to, even criminologists – especially criminologists (Kendall and Wickham, 2000: 30). Both methods of Archaeology and Genealogy are each other's accompaniment. By employing both, the result is an emphatic yet simplistic demystification of the here and now, whereby the fog of the present is dissipated.

Problems of the Present while Emphasizing Power

The method does not instruct observers of social phenomenon on what to look for, but the method does instruct observers on how to look. History, for the practitioner of the method, is central to employing the Genealogies and Archaeologies that investigate the many different discursive practices that involve "... a complex mix of success and failure which often involves the ingredient known widely, but fairly loosely, by the name resistance" (Kendall and Wickham, 2000: 32).

According to Foucault (1980: 142), "... there are no relations of power without resistance." In other words, if resistance does not exist, the expression of power requires the invention of resistance. Once resistance does exist, its strength must become the object of official exaggeration by the power that opposes it. Thus, the power of the state ceremoniously embellishes, strengthens, and – most importantly – legitimizes its own ability to crush resistance (i.e., exercise its power). In this way, power idealizes, deifies, worships, and most importantly, reproduces itself.

The Method's Fourth Cornerstone: Discursive Analysis

The fourth cornerstone of Kendall and Wickham's prescriptive method employs discursive analysis to transform systems of knowledge into ordered frameworks, whereby statements (e.g., us and them statements) are examined. In general, Kendall and Wickham consider discursive analysis to be a methodological mechanism or tool. According to these authors, researchers may use discursive analysis to:

> . . . illustrate, articulate, illuminate and make available to us the highly contested and unstable borderline between the normal and the abnormal in order to demonstrate the strangeness of the present and past (Kendall and Wickham, 2000: 35-9).

For Kendall and Wickham (2000: 42), researchers interested in conducting discursive analysis must satisfy five criteria as they conduct their research. In other words, to "do" discursive analysis, researchers must: 1) identify the rules of the production of statements, 2) recognize a discourse as a corpus of statements whose organization is regular and systematic, 3) identify rules that delimit the "sayable," 4) identify rules that ensure that a practice is material and discursive, and lastly 5) identify rules that create the spaces where new statements can be made. Before providing further explanations of how these criterion can be satisfied, a brief illustration of what discourse is **not** must enter into the discussion. Discourse is **not** another word for language. While discourse relates to language, discourse and language are not equivalent terms, primarily because "discourses are productive" (Kendall and Wickham, 2000: 34).

Identify the Rules of the Production of Statements

So what does discourse produce, and what are the rules of production? Among other things, a discourse produces statements (i.e., "sayable" statements and visible statements). Therefore, the first criterion to satisfy for researchers "doing" a discursive analysis is to identify the rules that govern the production of such statements. To illustrate, an example utilizing the discursive production of the "drug user" statement may prove valuable. At this point, the distinction between a "drug user" from a "person who uses drugs" must enter into the discussion.

For us, a person who "uses drugs" may be a grandfather who takes Viagra® or a child who takes Tylenol for a cold. A "person who uses drugs" may take caffeine in the morning to wake up quickly. The "person who uses drugs" may be the high school student who puffs on her/his cigarettes before a pep rally, mildly deviant, but one of us nonetheless. The "people who use drugs" are "us" and "drug users" are "them." The "person who uses drugs" is a person, whereas, the "drug user" is a not a person but a "user," a social construct.

The "drug user" is one of them. The "drug user" is a member (i.e., "abnormal" member) of society that abuses his/her membership by taking advantage of us (who, ironically, almost all use drugs, but legally), who are working hard and paying taxes. The "drug user" uses his or her membership into the great artificially extended family structure of American citizenship to defraud us (i.e., the normal) of our communal contributions (i.e. taxes), collective sense of morality (i.e., justice), and sense of well-being (i.e., safety).

As one of them (i.e., one of the abnormal), the worst-case scenario is often implied or projected upon the "drug user," and the most evil of human behaviors are attached to the "drug user." For example, by engaging in a selfish and hedonistic behavior, the "drug user" may also induce the self-destruction of the young, innocent, and inexperienced Americans (i.e., our children), encouraging their engagement in what only a few would say is something other than pure "evil." For evil is, I would argue, the very definition of them (i.e., "drug users"). For example, in 1988, Mario Cuomo, the Governor of the State of New York, told the children of a local school that he was proud of them for taking a stand against drugs, which he called "the devil." He stated, "Thank you from the bottom of my heart . . . Anybody who does not believe in the devil, think about drugs" (Szasz, 1992: 33). In summation, one of the discursive rules about drugs in America may be that "drug users" are evil and "people that use drugs" are good.

Recognize a Discourse as a Corpus (or Quantity) of Statements Whose Organization is Regular and Systematic

To illustrate what researchers are required to do, to satisfy the second criterion associated with conducting a discursive analysis, I use two analytical tools (i.e., the Archaeology of marijuana criminalization and the Genealogy of marijuana medicalization). The first analytical tool, the Archaeology, examines statements that tend to support the criminalization of marijuana. In this fashion, the Archaeology recognizes a quantity of statements associated with the discourse of marijuana criminalization in America, from the 1900s into the 1980s. In addition, the Archaeology of marijuana criminalization recognizes that the organization of these statements is standard and methodical. These statements tend to emphasize the dangers associated with marijuana use. For example, "Marijuana is addictive. Marijuana hurts young bodies and minds. Marijuana affects learning and academic achievement. Marijuana impairs driving. Marijuana today is stronger than ever. Marijuana users are younger today than ever" (ONDCP, 2004).

The second analytical tool, the Genealogy, examines statements that tend to support the medicalization of marijuana. In this fashion, the Genealogy recognizes a quantity of statements associated with the discourse of marijuana medicalization in America, from 1996 to 2004. In addition, the Genealogy of marijuana medicalization recognizes that the organization of these statements is standard and methodical. These statements tend to emphasize the benefits, or at least the harmlessness, associated with marijuana use. For example, "Marijuana is not harmful to health. Marijuana's therapeutic uses are well documented in the scientific literature. Marijuana does not cause physical dependence. Marijuana does not permanently impair memory and cognition. Marijuana use during pregnancy has no reliable impact on the fetus" (Zimmer and Morgan, 1997).

Identify Rules that Delimit the "Sayable"

To satisfy the third criterion associated with conducting a discursive analysis, researchers are required to recognize the set of rules that draw up the boundaries of the "sayable." For example, the discourse of marijuana criminalization consistently emphasizes one unofficial rule that draws up the boundaries of the "sayable" (i.e., all marijuana use is abuse). Conversely, the discourse of marijuana medicalization consistently emphasizes one unofficial rule that draws up the boundaries of the "sayable" (i.e., marijuana has medical value). In sum, the discourse of marijuana criminalization emphasizes that only bad/evil things come from marijuana, while the discourse of marijuana medicalization emphasizes that marijuana use is either harmless or therapeutic (i.e., beneficial/good).

Identify Rules that ensure that a Practice is Material and Discursive

To illustrate what researchers must do to satisfy the fourth criterion, I present an example of a "practice" that is both discursive and "material." At the federal level, marijuana is classified as a Schedule I drug (i.e., a drug with no medical value). This, by definition, moves the drug out of a medical sphere of authority and sustains the criminalization of the drug at the federal level. This has the effect of reproducing its label of illegitimacy, regardless of the many different state legalization ballot initiatives passing across the country. Since, federal law supersedes state law; even the use of state sanctioned medicinal marijuana is still officially a crime.

The discursive practice described above has material consequences. For example, the FBI-Uniform Crime Report entitled "Crime in the United States 2002" provides an account of the number of individuals encountering the criminal-justice system on drug charges involving marijuana. In 2002, the FBI reported that there were 1.5 million drug arrests in America. Of the total number of drug-related arrests, 80 percent (or 1.2 million) of the arrests were for simple possession. Marijuana made up nearly half (or 693,000) of all the arrests. Simple marijuana possession constituted nearly 88 percent (or approximately 610,000) of the arrests (FBI, 2003). In sum, marijuana's official definition of having no medical value does, in every year, materially impact numerous people as they receive the label of criminal for possessing and/or using marijuana.

Identify Rules that Create the Spaces where New Statements can be Made

To demonstrate what researchers must do to satisfy the fifth and final criterion associated with conducting a discursive analysis, I present an example of a rule associated with the creation of "spaces" or places that create new statements. The passage of the Federal Anti-Drug Legislation of 1988 resulted in a significant increase in the construction of new federal prisons, as well as the number federal prisoners incarcerated within these spaces. "Within six years, the number of drug cases in federal prisons increased by 300 percent. From 1986 to 1998 it was up by 450 percent" (Bikel, 1999). In part, the impact made by this legislation was that low-level traffickers could receive extremely harsh sentences if they refused to testify against another person. As a result, prosecutors gave even more encouragement to defendants to cut deals and manipulate the mandatory minimum sentencing laws (Bikel, 1999). Over time, defendants' accusations began to snowball – more accusations/statements brought in more defendants who were encouraged to make even more accusations/statements. As a result, the federal prison population began to swell and the government built more federal prisons (i.e., places) to accommodate the increasing population.

Summary

This chapter summarizes Kendall and Wickham's prescriptive methodological guide for research into historical analysis and reinterpretation, by discussing the four cornerstones of Kendall and Wickham's method (i.e., history, Archaeology, Genealogy, and discourse) and the criteria associated with each cornerstone. The first cornerstone of history specifies four criteria: 1) "problematise" history, 2) spot contingencies, 3) be skeptical of all political arguments, and 4) suspend second order judgments (Kendall and Wickham, 2000: 22-3). The second cornerstone of Archaeology specifies eight criteria that researchers are required to satisfy by describing: 1) statements in the archive that cover the visible and "sayable", 2) regularities of statements, 3) relations between one statement and other statements, 4) the formulation for the rules for the repeatability or use of statements, 5) positions which are established between subjects, 6) surfaces of emergence, 7) institutions which acquire authority and provide limits, and 8) forms of speculation (Kendall and Wickham, 2000: 24-8).

For the third cornerstone of Genealogy, researchers are required to describe: 1) and analyze disreputable origins and unpalatable functions, 2) power through the history of the present, 3) and make uncomfortable existing analyses, 4) statements as motion pictures or as an ongoing practice, 5) the web of discourse, and 6) problems of the present while emphasizing power (Kendall and Wickham, 2000: 28-34). Lastly, the fourth cornerstone of discourse and its five criteria require researchers to identify: 1) the rules of the production of statements, 2) discourse as a corpus of statements whose organization is regular and systematic, 3) rules that delimit the "sayable," 4) rules that ensure that a practice is material and discursive, and lastly 5) rules that create the spaces where new statements can be made.

As long as researchers follow the above methodological prescriptions, Kendall and Wickham contend that researchers can produce surprising results. Such results are possible by creating better investigations. Through creating better investigations into objects of inquiry, Kendall and Wickham assert that their method guides researchers in how to look, not in what to look for. In summation, Kendall and Wickham encourage researchers to stop viewing historical research as the examination of static records of unquestionable past interpretations. In so doing, researchers may encourage their audience to do the same.

Chapter Four
Archaeology of Marijuana Criminalization

In this chapter, I use Archaeology as my tool to illustrate the discursive mechanisms of marijuana criminalization. By illustrating discursive mechanisms, I mean describing or specifying the frameworks by which power and knowledge get work done. By getting work done, I am referring to the way by which power and knowledge work together in an alliance through language and material actions to accomplish specific goals. These goals may involve the introduction, distribution, proliferation, and even destruction of new and pre-existing complexes of knowledge or systems of thought. Put another way, different discursive mechanisms are loosely comparable to different paradigms in systems of citizen control, or even different fashions of thought and conduct, within a collective of knowledge complexes. While one system of thought and action (i.e., system of domination) moves into vogue, another may be displaced or altered.

I describe the discursive mechanisms of criminalization in this chapter as a general history using Conrad and Schneider's theory to guide the investigation. The archive of statements and visibilities constitutes the body of evidence (or data) under investigation. The Archaeology provides the order by which the evidence of marijuana criminalization, as a historical process, finds appropriate methodological and theoretical connection. I specify congruencies, as well as their implicit incongruent counterparts, among other artifacts of the processual apparatus under scrutiny. Thus, allowing me to examine evidence of mutations in historical systems of thought.

This chapter also uses historical periods to bookend the subject matter of general historical inquiry. In so doing, I use the Archaeology of marijuana criminalization to analyze the framework of processual discourse. Simply put, I do not primarily look for the players on the pitch of marijuana criminalization; however, I do look at their statements. By examining statements made by people who lobbied and fought for the criminalization of marijuana, the analysis uncovers evidence of the general characteristics of processual discursive change (Kendall and Wickham, 2000: 25).

As I assess America's contemporary marijuana problem, continua develop. In addition, ideal types polarize from temperance to prohibition, vice to crime, self to collective and from moral indignation to legislative constraint. How did the present arrive here, where the United States has declared a war on a simple plant? Szasz believes that the story began nearly a century ago. He states:

> Thus, in 1906 it was illegal to operate a lottery, but it was legal to sell and buy heroin; today it is the other way around. Formally, gambling is considered to be a public service (indeed, it is a state monopoly, like the postal service), and playing the lottery is regarded as neither a vice nor a crime. (It is regarded as a disease only if the player loses too much money; then he suffers from "pathological.") My point is simply that neither participating in the drug trade nor using drugs (legal or illegal) need be interpreted as constituting vice, crime, or disease (Szasz, 1992: 44-45).

Using The Foucaultian Method, I do not focus attention on the continuities of different periods in American drug policy history. For example, the continuities within the criminalization of marijuana era (1906 to 1996) or the precriminalization of marijuana era (1776 to 1906) does not drive the analysis. Instead, I observe and comment on the quick and dramatic shifts in our systems of thought associated with the criminalization of marijuana in America throughout this chapter.

The consistencies found within the era of governmental marijuana prohibition have been the subjects of many articles, chapters, and books. The different forms of legislation that resulted from marijuana prohibition also receive ample analysis. However, scholars pay little attention to the quick fissures of activity that set the stage for America's long-term prohibition of marijuana. The method is an integral part of my study as I examine these brief and dramatic changes in the social history of marijuana. In addition, Conrad and Schneider, Foucault, and Currie implicitly drive my analysis by allowing my investigation to become and remain grounded in sociological theory.

In general, this study of the general history of criminalization and medicalization does not reduce systems of thought associated with one historical period or another. Instead, my analysis expands upon the rapid and definitive changes in systems of thought within the social history of marijuana in America (Kendall and Wickham, 2000: 24). More specifically, this chapter focuses on the rapid shifts in systems of thought about marijuana. As a result, this chapter focuses on several different and previously ignored contingencies that were closely associated with eight core legislative events. Understanding the relationships between these eight core legislative events and several different and specific contingencies, or accidents of history, allows me to better understand and document quick transitions in systems of thought. I argue that these quick transitions in systems of thought are historically significant as well as historically specific. Ultimately, these quick transitions in systems of thought are instrumental in the construction and destruction of major complexes of knowledge.

Kendall and Wickham define a contingency within the context of a Foucaultian analysis as an accident of history. They state:

> When we describe a historical event as contingent, what we mean is that the emergence of that event was not necessary but was one possible result of a whole series of complex relations between other events . . . The problem is, most of us get into the habit of looking for causes. We need to break this habit in favour of the easier move of accepting them as contingencies (Kendall and Wickham, 2000: 5-6).

The history of American drug policy has recently emerged into the mainstream of academic and trade press as scholars increasingly acknowledge the strangeness of America's fight against marijuana. Nevertheless, the past may best assist us in understanding our strange present. For example, in *The Eighteenth*

Brumaire of Louis Bonaparte, Karl Marx made the point that social actors must not only play the hand that history dealt them, but they must also accept that their present is a product of the past. Marx stated that human beings:

> [M]ake their own history [b]ut do not make it just as they please; they do not make it under circumstances chosen by themselves, but under circumstances directly encountered, given and transmitted from the past. The tradition of all dead generations weighs like a nightmare on the brain of the living (Marx, 1963/1852: 15).

The cultural baggage associated with the topic of marijuana is immense. My analysis is not only driven by the social history of this plant for its mystique, but also by the lack of understanding that seems to surround this powerful symbol of postmodern counterculture.

The Archaeology
First Core Legislative Event: The Pure Food and Drug Act of 1906

The Wiley Act of 1906 is the same as the Federal Pure Food and Drug Act of 1906. Because it was passed with little fanfare or discussion, the Act now stands as a monument to all uncontroversial and banal legislation. Its summary reads:

> An act for preventing the manufacture, sale, or transportation of adulterated or misbranded or poisonous or deleterious foods, drugs, medicines, and liquors, and for regulating traffic therein, and for other purposes (FDA, 2004).

In hindsight and a century later, I cannot overemphasize the understated power of the 1906 Act. While the 1906 Act was not an important contingency as a stand-alone document, it was the first step toward the erosion of some of Americans' most closely guarded civil liberties. Contemporary scholars such as Thomas Szasz now view the 1906 Act as "the foot in the door of paternalistic-statist protectionism." He states:

Although in some respects the Food and Drug Act of 1906 was a salutatory piece of legislation because it increased the consumer's power to make an informed choice in the market, its enactment enabled the federal government to enter an arena where the utmost vigilance was required to contain its power. However, such a paranoid posture toward therapeutic state paternalism was by that time quite unfashionable (Szasz, 1992: 38-39).

My analysis views the Wiley Act of 1906 as a contingency, nothing more and nothing less. It is a contingency among many other contingencies that made possible (but did not cause) the classification scheme of marijuana to change from an herbal and legal remedy to a deviant and harmful drug. More importantly, the 1906 Act was a contingency that marked the beginning of the federal government's century long journey to eviscerate the nation's Tenth Amendment.

Second Core Legislative Event: The Harrison Narcotics Act of 1914

The second legislative event associated with the historical drift of marijuana into its criminal designation was the passage of the Harrison Act of 1914. Its summary reads:

An act to provide for the registration of, with collectors of internal revenue, and to impose a special tax on all persons who produce, import, manufacture, compound, deal in, dispense, sell, distribute, or give away opium or coca leaves, their salts, derivatives, or preparations, and for other purposes (Schaffer Library of Drug Policy, 2004).

Specifically created to regulate the opium and coca markets, the 1914 Act also included marijuana under its umbrella. Part of the prohibitory push associated with marijuana during this period came from efforts to suppress the importation and subsequent distribution of what the local deputy sheriff of El Paso, Texas, in 1914, began calling locoweed. The deputy sheriff argued that Mexicans were bringing the plant into the United States and asked the federal government to take what some legal scholars (Bonnie and Whitebread, 1970: 13) refer to as "the only available administrative action." The action included asking the Secretary of Agriculture to do something about the problem. The Secretary soon declared the very existence of the plant a social problem. The Secretary of Agriculture stated, with respect to the importation of marijuana across the Mexican/American border, "[marijuana is] being used for purposes other than in the preparation of medicines and that, unless used in medicinal preparations, this drug is believed to be injurious to health" (Bonnie and Whitebread, 1987: 14).

In 1914, the Internal Revenue Commissioner asked that marijuana be included in the Harrison Act. This addition to the Act attracted little attention before or after the passage of the Act (Bonnie and Whitebread, 1987: 14). While the Harrison Act officially prohibited Americans from recreationally using marijuana, without the passage of The Pure Food and Drug Act of 1906, The Harrison Act of 1914 could never have included marijuana. The Pure Food and Drug Act of 1906 gave the Secretary of the Treasury authority to deny the importation of the drug into America if it was not specifically for medicinal purposes. Seizing on this point, scholars such as R. Bonnie and C. H. Whitebread (1987) question the constitutionality of the regulatory responses to marijuana. They state:

> The Harrison Narcotics Act was drafted as a tax law rather than an outright regulatory or prohibitory statute in order to accomplish indirectly what Congress believed, probably correctly, it could not do directly, - that is to regulate the possession and sale of narcotics. That the Supreme Court upheld the act as an exercise of taxing power by a slim five to four margin in 1919 [and] had a significant bearing on the federal response to marijuana during the ensuing twenty years. In 1930 the narcotics area of the Prohibition Bureau's responsibilities were extracted (from the Treasury Department) and transferred to a separate Bureau of Narcotics (Bonnie and Whitebread, 1970: 14).

After the passage of the Harrison Act, buying or selling of marijuana for non-medicinal purposes was prohibited at the federal level. At this time, the end run around most constitutional barriers associated with the federal prohibition of all forms of marijuana was partially complete. Even so, I emphasize that the total prohibition of medicinal marijuana was not complete at this point in history.

It would take an optional provision, in 1932, to bring marijuana into the Uniform Narcotic Drug Act. By this action, the attention of the American middle class, who had just frustrated the national campaign to prohibit alcohol, was artfully avoided (Bonnie and Whitebread, 1970). To restate, the end of alcohol prohibition was a very important contingency that set the stage for the beginning of overt marijuana prohibition.

Third Core Legislative Event: The Uniform Narcotic Drug Act (1932)

After the passage of the Harrison Act, any buying or selling of marijuana outside of official medical purposes was illegal at the federal level. As a result, the official prohibition of recreational marijuana use at the federal level represented a new and official criminal designation. The everyday prohibition of marijuana, medicinal or otherwise, had yet to embed in the minds of all citizens. The very word *marijuana* had yet to reflect its most recent and taboo classification. To accomplish such an aim, a moral entrepreneur emerged.

A brilliant claims maker by the name of Harry J. Anslinger literally, over the course of a decade (1927-1937), seized all statements associated with marijuana and transformed the very meaning of these statements. Anslinger began with the transformation of the very word marihuana. He understood that as statements become legitimate, they must undergo repetition over time. As the reproduction of statements occur on a mass scale, they become increasingly salient and prominent. In this way, statements are more likely to enter into reproduction for others to encounter and process. Simply put, Anslinger understood that for a naïve and gullible public, repetition could create a new truth brand. This is how Anslinger, single-handedly, altered the pronunciation of the word marihuana to marijuana (i.e., "mara-wanna" to "marry-JUAN-na") as the word entered into the public arena of play. Anslinger artfully privileged the Mexican slang pronunciation of marijuana with a "j" over the Americanized pronunciation of marihuana with an "h." Overtime, Anslinger associated the plant with the Hispanic population.

Jack Herer clarifies a power relationship between the Americanized word marihuana and the slang Mexican word marijuana in the following quote:

> Hearst [Anslinger's newspaper tycoon associate], through pervasive and repetitive use, pounded the obscure Mexican slang word 'marijuana' into the English-speaking American consciousness. 'Hemp' was discarded. 'Cannabis,' the scientific term, was ignored or buried. The actual Spanish word for hemp is 'canamo.' But using a Mexican Sonoran colloquialism – marijuana, often Americanized as 'marihuana' – guaranteed that no one would realize the world's chief natural medicine and premier industrial resource had been outflanked, outlawed and pushed out of the language (Herer, 1985: 25).

Over time, Anslinger, through his position, began to oversee the emergence of a new federal bureaucracy, the Federal Narcotics Bureau (FNB). Nevertheless, before he could publicly exercise the power of the newly formed FNB, Anslinger's fledgling agency first needed subjects to capture and control. Minority subjects, who were politically disadvantaged, appeared to be Anslinger's primary targets. To accomplish his aims, Anslinger's association with the newspaper tycoon William Randolph Hearst proved to be of great value. Anslinger would profit most if the everyday language about marijuana would change, not just the officially codified norms about marijuana. Since Anslinger could effortlessly deliver animated and outrageous tales about the horrors of marijuana, Hearst profited by selling more newspapers and magazines through displaying Anslinger's claims making prowess. Hence, the Anslinger-Hearst relationship proved to be a reciprocal one.

Hearst and Anslinger were a formidable force to reckon with. While Anslinger provided the charismatic leadership needed to move the masses into a small but sustainable moral panic, Hearst held the power to publish and mass-produce Anslinger's incendiary rhetoric into the truth by way of the printed page, causing small moral panics to snowball into nationwide scares.

Radio was also an important medium. For example, the World Narcotics Defense Association sponsored a four-part prohibition series, which assisted

Anslinger in creating and sustaining the marijuana panic. The Congressional Record of March 5, 1935 printed one of these radio broadcasts. The title of the broadcast was, "Law Versus the Narcotic Drug Evil." Making the argument for an interstate accord on narcotics, the broadcast admonishes all of the states to adopt the Uniform Narcotic Drug Act. The radio series contained an address by H.J. Anslinger. I quote a small portion of Anslinger's address below:

> At the 1931 conference great strides were taken by agreement upon terms for effective limitation of the manufacture of narcotic drugs to the actual needs of mankind, for scientific and medicinal purposes, and for strict control of the drugs manufactured for these purposes so that none of them would find their way into the channels of illicit trade. The treaty that evolved by that conference constitutes the most powerful blow that has thus far been dealt to the illicit narcotic traffic. This treaty is now the basis of international accord on narcotics. Indeed, the Limitation Treaty of 1931 may properly be called the Magna Carta of world freedom from the narcotic drug tyrant. Internationally, the allied forces in the warfare on the narcotic drug evil have achieved great victories, and are now consolidated in a strong position, well prepared for the next offensive. In the United States, however, there is weakness in the lines of defense against this enemy of all mankind (Congressional Record, 1935).

Before Anslinger started to speak into the microphone to deliver the above words, the vice president of the World Narcotics Defense Association introduced Anslinger as "the able, faithful, and efficient United States Commissioner of Narcotics – the chief federal official of the national narcotic laws and treaties." By the end of 1937, almost all of the states had adopted the Uniform Narcotics Act.

While Anslinger was one of the more important claims makers, Hearst was not his sole assistant. The World Narcotics Defense Association used press and radio very effectively to supply the statements necessary to create anti-marijuana visibilities. By create anti-marijuana visibilities, I mean that the American public needed indoctrination in anti-drug propaganda before they would be able to identify the marijuana user in their own communities. Through Anslinger and Hearst, the American public learned that most of these marijuana users were identifiable by the color of their skin. The use of popular press and radio to distribute anti-drug hype and information helped Anslinger's campaign to gain momentum. A small portion of a 1937 New York Times article, "World Group to Push Fight on Marijuana: Illicit Drug to be Chief Target of Week's Narcotic Fight Opening Today," reads:

> With special emphasis on the increasing use of marijuana in the United States, the World Narcotics Defense Association all this week will observe the eleventh annual Narcotic Educational Week, appealing to the public through the press and radio as well as through religious, fraternal and educational institutions. The association will campaign for the enactment of the Uniform State Narcotic Drug Act in the District of Columbia and fifteen States, for efficient narcotic law enforcement and prompt and effective action against violators by the courts and for more thorough instruction in schools concerning dangerous narcotic drugs. The campaign will be on a national scale (NYT, 1937).

As statements, such as the one above, produce and reproduce the efforts of the powerful, statements become situated and positioned as true as an increasingly fearful public look to political leaders for solutions. How these testimonials are fashioned, conveyed, and made into replicas is of import to my analysis (Kendall and Wickham, 2000: 24).

Before 1906, using the plant was not openly into public view as deviant. In fact, it was widely recommended by physicians to treat various ailments and syndromes. Nevertheless, by 1920, moral entrepreneurs like Capt. Richmond Hobson were taking an uncompromising and unreflective stance against marijuana use for any reason whatsoever. Richard Hobson was the president of the International Narcotic Education Association and the World Narcotic Defense Association. Hobson was a former Congressman and a Spanish-American War hero, as well as a highly influential temperance activist.

> Hobson . . . became involved in the campaign against the 'dope traffic' in 1920. That year, he helped get a twenty-five page textbook for teachers written and distributed, so that schoolchildren could be warned about the dangers of narcotic addiction. Following this he

helped establish several anti-narcotic organizations: the International Narcotic Education Association in 1923, the World Conference on Narcotic Education in 1926, and the World Narcotic Defense Organization in 1927. These groups worked hard to raise public awareness, using many of the tactics that had worked so well for the Anti-Saloon League and Woman's Christian Temperance Union against alcohol: enlisting the aid of prominent citizens (e.g. physicians, attorneys, judges, and legislators) and civic organizations, holding national and international conferences, agitating for stricter controls, and sponsoring Narcotic Education Week during the last week in February beginning in 1927. They sent out (by Hobson's account) millions of pamphlets and article reprints, contributed articles to magazines and newspapers, and contacted teachers and school superintendents (Speaker, 2001: 3).

Claims-makers such as Hobson emphasized the interconnections of individual and group alliances that moved to illustrate the plant as evil, in and of itself. Thereby, the plant's meaning underwent transformation, away from the organic, material and natural (i.e. normal).

Fourth Core Legislative Event: The Marijuana Tax Act of 1937

By 1937, the plant was well on its way to notoriety and infamy. Nevertheless, it was the passage of the Marijuana Tax Act of 1937, which transformed bad into crime. The Act did not designate marijuana at the federal level as medically useless or unusable. Nevertheless, the Marijuana Tax Act of 1937 did make buying, selling, and even growing the plant virtually impossible. To emphasize, the Marijuana Tax Act of 1937 did not make marijuana illegal, to buy or sell, but the Act did make it difficult to produce, market, and distribute *cannabis* through the imposition of a prohibitive tax. The method of creating a tax, not for the purpose of generating revenue for the federal government, but to regulate behavior was, at first, something of a silent yet controversial topic in 1937. Herer illustrates:

In the secret Treasury Department meetings conducted between 1935 and 1937, prohibitive tax laws were drafted and strategies plotted. 'Marijuana' was not banned outright; the law called for an 'occupational excise tax upon dealers, and a transfer tax upon dealings in marijuana.' Importers, manufacturers, sellers and distributors were required to register with the Secretary of the Treasury and pay the occupational tax. Transfers were taxed at $1 an ounce; $100 an ounce if the dealer was unregistered. The new tax doubled the price of the legal 'raw drug' cannabis which at the time sold for one dollar an ounce. The year was 1937. New York State had exactly one narcotics officer. After the Supreme Court decision of March 29, 1937, upholding the prohibition of machine guns through taxation, Herman Oliphant made his move. On April 14, 1937 he introduced the bill directly to the House Ways and Means Committee instead of to other appropriate committees such as Food and Drug, Agriculture, Textiles, Commerce, etc. His reason may have been that 'Ways and Means' is the only committee that can send its bills directly to the House floor without being subject to debate by other committees. Ways and Means Chairman Robert L. Doughton, a key DuPont ally, quickly rubber-stamped the secret Treasury bill and sent it sailing through Congress to the President (Herer, 1985: 25-26).

This Act was the introduction of the federal prohibition of marijuana, but marijuana criminalization had entered in through the back door, to avoid any Constitutional safeguards that might have made for an awkward exchange of legitimacies. To restate, the Supreme Court's decision to uphold the prohibition of machine guns, through a prohibitive tax, was another important contingency that set the stage for the beginning of overt marijuana prohibition.

The origins of federal marijuana prohibition were, in a word, disreputable. Nevertheless, in 1937 things changed abruptly in American drug policy discourse. This period was a time of building tensions associated with public policy on medicinal and recreational marijuana. As a result, the way by which America's health and criminal justice systems viewed marijuana underwent transformation. By April 1937, the Ways and Means Committee of the U.S. House of Representatives held hearings on H.R. 6385, the Marijuana Tax Act of 1937. Not long after, with little fanfare or debate and only a modicum of public attention, Congress passed the legislation (Herer, 1985: 25-26).

There was much misinformation spread during the passage of this legislation. During the House Hearings, Assistant General Counsel for the Treasury Department, Fred Vinson, gave false testimony by claiming that the bill received support from the

American Medical Association, although the AMA had specifically voiced disapproval of the bill. Also significant is the fact that members of the United States government had acted in concert with powerful and influential U.S. big business interests during this time. These big business interests included William Randolph Hearst, Andrew Mellon, as well as Lammot DuPont, President of the DuPont Chemical Corporation (Herer, 1985: 25-26).

Anslinger was working behind the scenes with William Randolph Hearst (newspaper and magazine tycoon), Andrew Mellon (Chairman of Mellon Bank and founder of the Gulf Oil Corporation), and Lammot DuPont (President of the DuPont Chemical Corporation).[1] Anslinger was an in-law of the Mellons and received an

---

[1] DuPont mentioned in a 1937, through a company annual report addressed to his stockholders, whereby he "…strongly urged action (investment) despite the economic chaos of the Great Depression. DuPont was anticipating 'radical changes' from 'the revenue raising power of government… converted into an instrument for forcing acceptance of sudden new ideas of industrial and social reorganization'" (Herer,1985: 24).

   While historical accidents may never reveal their alternatives, hemp activist and citizen scholar, Jack Herer (1985: 24) speculates as to the meaning behind DuPont's annual report recommendations.
   In DuPont's 1937 Annual Report to its stockholders, the company strongly urged continued investment in its new, but not readily accepted, petrochemical synthetic products . . . Coincidentally, in 1937, DuPont had just patented processes for making plastics from oil and coal, as well as a new sulfate/sulfite process for making paper from wood pulp . . . If hemp had not been made illegal, 80% of DuPont's business would never have materialized . . . But competing against environmentally-sane hemp paper and natural plastic technology would have jeopardized the lucrative financial schemes of Hearst, DuPont and DuPont's chief financial backer, Andrew Mellon of the Mellon Bank of Pittsburgh . . . In 1931, Mellon, in his role as Hoover's Secretary of the Treasury, appointed his future nephew-in-law, Harry J. Anslinger, to be head of the newly reorganized Federal Bureau of Narcotics and Dangerous Drugs (FBNDD), a post he held for the next 31 years . . . These industrial barons and financiers knew that machinery to cut, bale, decorticate (separate the fiber from the high-cellulose hurd), and process hemp into paper or plastics was becoming available in the mid-1930s. *Cannabis* hemp would have to go (Herer 1985: 24).

Herer envisions an alternative history for Americans – an alternative future in which today's petrochemical dystopia "could have been" replaced by an environmentally conscious hemp industry.

   Even today, the "Hearst-Du Pont-Mellon" affiliation is often unquestioned and referred to as a "conspiracy" by many of the medicinal marijuana activists and nonprofit marijuana decriminalization organizations. The "Hearst-Du Pont-Mellon Conspiracy Theory," while processing a certain amount of *je ne se qua*, is not a fruitful line of inquiry to pursue at the current juncture. A past reality such as a "Hearst-Du Pont-Mellon Conspiracy" is just as likely (and uninteresting) as a contemporary reality such as a "Bush-Bush W.-Cheney-Halliburton Conspiracy." The past, I contend, is just as banal and strange as the present.

   The primary distinction between 1937 and present day in America may very well be in the way we interpret our surroundings and the information that surrounds us as Americans. Modernity characterized America in 1937 and post-modernity characterizes America today. In giving a hypothetical illustration, I temporarily play Herer's game of envisioning alternative histories. For

appointment to a position of leadership within the newly founded Federal Bureau of Narcotics by Mellon. Mellon was, during that period, the Secretary of the U.S. Treasury. In addition, Mellon secured a loan for DuPont to take over General Motors during the 1920s (Herer, 1985: 25-26).

The Hearst-DuPont-Mellon affiliation is often unquestioned but referred to as a conspiracy by many contemporary medicinal marijuana activists. Many of these activists are now working for nonprofit marijuana decriminalization organizations that are currently operating out of today's beltway of power and political discourse, Washington, D.C. The Hearst-DuPont-Mellon "conspiracy," while possessing a certain amount of appeal is inconsequential for the purposes of the inquiry at hand. The idea that members of the U.S. government acted in concert with powerful and influential capitalist interests in the past was not only likely, but also imperative. This was necessary for the continued reproduction of the capitalist state and its past, and current, mechanisms for regulating the behavior of its citizens. I am not claiming that relationships among the politically and fiscally powerful in America are always ethical or moral; then again, I am not claiming that they are always unethical and immoral. For example, DuPont and his corporation were not conspiring to make marijuana (i.e., hemp) illegal in America. DuPont and his corporation were outwardly lobbying to eliminate industrial hemp as a natural resource. DuPont's corporation had invented plastic and was looking to open up a market for their new petroleum based product. In addition, DuPont's corporation had produced a low cost method for chemically treating timber for the production of

---

example, had the U.S. invaded a country like Iraq (in 1937) much of the perception from the mainstream media would not have questioned the authority and legitimacy of America and Americans to colonize another "lesser developed" nation like Iraq. Today, the legitimacy and authority of America and Americans to do the very same thing is in question.

Today, Americans expect political and fiscal power brokers to be corrupt, however, within the framework of a very "modernist 1937" most Americans may have assumed that politicians represented the best interests of "the people" rather than the capitalist elite...which by the way are also "people" living at that time in America. In summation, while it is entertaining to speculate and it is certainly tempting to demonize the likes of "industrial barons" such as Anslinger, DuPont, Mellon, and Hearst...such speculations about "conspiracies" are inconsequential to my present investigation. However, the evidence does suggest that there was organized capitalist interest associated with the elimination of hemp from the marketplace. In this manner, these circumstances do represent an important contingency to consider.

paper. To prohibit marijuana would eliminate DuPont's competition, America's hemp industry.

It is important to realize and clarify that the Marijuana Tax Act of 1937 did not criminalize the cultivation, harvest, distribution, and subsequent sale of marijuana. It did essentially make the production, use, and sale of the plant nearly impossible. If one could somehow grow the plant without the stems, leaves, and flowers (i.e., buds) then one did not have to pay the excessive and unwarranted tax. After all, one hundred dollars was a large sum of money back in 1937. Marijuana became so impractical and cost prohibitive to grow legally, it moved into the black market overnight and soon fell within the federal domain of regulatory methods, involving coercive mechanisms of official control and prohibition.[2] Those who

---

[2] It may be helpful to view the first third of the twentieth century as a period of building tensions between the fault lines of public policy discourse on medicinal and recreation marijuana, as well as the production and manufacture of hemp and all of its related uses. In 1937, the tension could no longer build and the plates fractured at their fault lines, violently shifting under the sea of American drug policy discourse. As a result, the way by which America's health and criminal justicesystems view the use of one of the world's most celebrated, and hated creations of nature would be irrevocably transformed.

Having said as much, the method would instruct me to pause at the present juncture and emphasize that both arguments (positioned around the passage of the 1937 legislation) are neither true nor false. However, both do coexist within the same temporal/special location and one argument demonstrates more power, creating more belief. The power to create "legitimated" belief is a lynch pin issue which emerges and connects these two arguments.

The disparate impact of information and misinformation on creating belief is not subject to an empirical fact tally. For the Foucaultian observer, fact and fiction hold equal footing as public opinion sways in one direction or another, issue by issue, and time after time. It matters not whether one argument captures some sort of absolute truth or some sort of unknowable set of facts. It is of more interest to the observer using the Foucaultian method to find out how these moral entrepreneurs get their work done. How do these charismatic individuals get so many citizens to "buy" what they, as moral entrepreneurs, are selling?

The moral entrepreneurs are "selling" their own solution to the newly illuminated symptoms of their particularly defined "social problem." They have invented a means to their ends. In this manner, they succeed in creating the urgency and need for the status quo to pursue their own agenda, as bureaucratic expansion of professional turf canonizes the moral entrepreneur's cult of personality. Sheldon and Brown (2003: 196) call the previously described phenomena as the "edifice complex." They illustrate below:

Indeed, we have continued to succumb to what can be called the edifice complex. This refers to the fact that we have continued to view the solution to many human problems as requiring some form of "edifice" – a courthouse, an institution, a detention center. Yet at the same time, we have succumbed to the Field of Dreams Syndrome– "If you build them, they will come," In other words, as soon as you construct these edifices, they will be filled almost immediately.

In fairness, many criminologists and sociologists have the precise solutions in mind as they

failed to pay the tax could then be subject to arrest for federal tax evasion (Baum, 1996: 22-23).

The Kendall and Wickham method uses an action-based Archaeology to scrutinize the affiliation between the sayable and the visible. With respect to The Marijuana Tax Act of 1937, the sayable within the context of the analysis can illustrate the yellow journalism associated with some of the Hearst publications. Jack Herer, a contemporary hemp activist, captured some of the Hearst headlines in his book, *The Emperor Wears No Clothes* (Herer, 1985: 25). Headlines used by Hearst include:

- Marihuana Makes Fiends of Boys in 30 Days
- Hasheesh Goads Users to Blood Lust
- New Dope Lure, Marijuana, has many Victims
- Hotel Clerk Identifies Marihuana Smoker as 'Wild Gunman' Arrested for Shootings
- Crusade against Marihuana

A portion of *Crusade against Marijuana*, originally published in America in the mid-1930s is below. The article illustrates the fear-based logic of a moral entrepreneur engaged in the active use of misinformation. In so doing, the moral entrepreneur creates the impression of an epidemic of immorality. The newspaper article sounds the alarm in part because appearing in print legitimates the message. The article shocks and scares the reader into accepting the existence of an epidemic of immorality. It asserts that criminally "insane" marihuana smoking boys committed the vast majority of the "atrocious crimes blotting the daily picture of American life" (Herer, 1985: 25).

---

investigate, "uncover" and move to define a new "social problem" taking credit for its "discovery" in the privileging of their citations in subsequent works or by affixing their name to the problem or the solution to the problem.

While most sociologists and criminologists do not have prisons or libraries named after them, many are well aware of their research "answers" before they have posed their research questions. In their defense, very few laypersons look for something when they are unaware that they have lost in the first place. I would contend that, as researchers looking for new and exciting forms of knowledge, we might best look for meaning in, not how knowledge is "lost or found" but rather, in how knowledge is bought and sold (or produced and consumed) not just fiscally but ideologically, morally, and politically.

A nationwide crusade of American women against the menace of marijuana smoking has been launched by the Women's National Exposition of Arts and Industries in New York City. H. J. Anslinger, head of the Federal Narcotics Bureau, explained to the group the urgent necessity of NATIONAL ACTION. Declaring that marijuana smoking is 'taking our youth like wildfire' Mr. Anslinger said: 'If the hideous monster Frankenstein came face to face with the monster marijuana he would drop dead of fright.' This is not an overstatement. Users of the marihuana weed are committing a large percentage of the atrocious crimes blotting the daily picture of American life. It is reducing thousands of boys to CRIMINAL INSANITY. And only two states have effective laws to protect their people against it. The marihuana weed, according to mister Anslinger is grown, sold and USED in every state in the Union. He charges, and rightly, that this is not a responsibility of one State, but OF ALL– and of the Federal Government. American women aroused to this DANGER, will GET ACTION. In New York State organized groups of women are GETTING ACTION by demanding the enactment of the McNaboe bill creating a State Narcotics Bureau. That Bureau would replace the existing one-man Narcotics Division, which is powerless to cope with the fact that eighty per cent [original spelling] of New York's criminals are narcotic addicts (all emphasis in original article) (Herer, 1985: 25).

Herer argues that Anslinger engaged in vigorous moral entrepreneurialism during the 1930s as he "went around the country giving speeches to judges, police, unions, etc., on the evils of marijuana" (Herer, 1985). The article's account of Anslinger's crusade reveals some popular themes among current anti-drug discursive mechanisms. The Hearst articles helped convince readers that marijuana prohibition fell within the legitimate sphere of federal law enforcement. The message was that citizens are expected to work in partnership with the federal government to combat the evils of "the narcotic" marijuana. At the same time, an argument that the state was not equipped to "protect their people against [marijuana]" became popular (Herer 1985: 25). Anslinger argued that not only were American citizens incapable of protecting themselves against the dangers of marijuana, but that the government itself was ill equipped to deal with the marijuana problem.

The Marijuana Tax Act of 1937 transformed marijuana from a legal substance into a criminal substance almost overnight. After 1937, the legal status of marijuana became murky for those who used to purchase the drug from their pharmacist and even for those who used to grow the herbal remedy and use it for self-medication. I conceptualize the end of marijuana's legal status as an event. To reexamine and shed light on this past event may allow me to investigate the modern day phenomena of marijuana medicalization with an understanding of the process of deviant designation change. To restate, I argue that it is possible to understand the current process of medicalization (of deviant designation change) through the study of past criminalization, as a similar process of deviant designation change.

Fifth Core Legislative Event: The Boggs Act of 1952

During the early 1950s, a number of rationales emerged that justified the introduction and passage of draconian anti-marijuana legislation. During this decade the predecessor of today's Gateway Theory (suggesting that marijuana use leads to abuse of other "harder" drugs) emerged. The 1950s witnessed the birth of an enormous coercive criminal justice system that continued to grow throughout the 1960s. Although it waned in popularity in the 1970s, it was reborn in the dramatic escalation of the anti-drug legislation of the 1980s, under the conservative Reagan and Bush presidencies. The 1950s also represented a decade naively optimistic about attempts to legislate deviant behavior away. Some scholars, such as Bonnie and Whitebread (1970), referred to these actions as "mindless escalation." By mindless escalation, they mean that making penalties more draconian is a mindless attempt by legislators to solve the marijuana problem.

Throughout the 1950s, the Federal Bureau of Narcotics' use of "classic nineteenth century police paradigm which applied localized coercion to the eradication of domestic vice trading" characterized marijuana prohibition (McCoy, 2004). One of the more fascinating and overlooked aspects of the Boggs Act Hearings of 1951 was the testimony of a physician named Dr. Harris Isbell. Isbell, the Director of Research at the Public Health Service Hospital in Lexington,

Kentucky, used his testimony as an opportunity to argue that marijuana was neither criminogenic, nor harmful to the health of users. Additionally, Dr. Isbell asserted that marijuana was not addictive and did not lead to the use of harder drugs. Nevertheless, The Boggs Act took marijuana "along for the ride" by indiscriminately lumping marijuana in with narcotics such as heroin (Bonnie and Whitebread, 1970).

Isbell's comments were confusing to the members of the Committee. He claimed that illicit hallucinogens (such as marijuana) or stimulants (such as cocaine or amphetamine) were no more marked for dependence than other licit stimulants (such as tobacco or coffee). Dr. Isbell went even further to blur the line between good and evil when he suggested responsible maintenance of an addiction to a dependent drug (such as morphine) did less harm to an individual's health than using nondependent drugs (such as marijuana and cocaine). At the time, Dr. Isbell was trying to clarify the difference between drugs that met the classic medical definition of addiction, and other drugs, that were powerfully reinforcing (psychologically) to the user but not physically addictive. Nevertheless, Dr. Isbell concluded it was best to keep the illicit physically nondependent drugs (such as marijuana and cocaine) on the "list of addicting drugs" to avoid "endless confusion because in common parlance and legally, both drugs are regarded as addicting" (Bonnie and Whitebread, 1970).

Dr. Isbell reluctantly posited that scientific knowledge should acquiesce to scientifically unsound legal definitions and the widespread vernacular associated with marijuana use. Nevertheless, both Anslinger and Isbell agreed within the context of what role a unified paternalist/therapeutic state should play in the production, regulation, and reproduction of marijuana using subjects. Here, medical definitions of addiction do not trump legal and colloquial definitions of addiction.

The following exchange between Representative Boggs and Commissioner Anslinger only partially summarizes the act:

> **Mr. Boggs**. From just what little I saw in that demonstration, I have forgotten the figure Dr. Isbell gave, but my recollection is that only

> a small percentage of those marijuana cases were anything more than
> a temporary degree of exhilaration . . .
> **Mr. Anslinger**. The danger is this: Over 50 percent of those young
> addicts started on marijuana smoking. They started there and
> graduated to heroin; they took the needle when the thrill of marijuana
> was gone (Bonnie and Whitebread, 1970).

Anslinger was not speaking science; he was speaking crime. Anslinger was politically motivated as he sought to criminalize marijuana. The act of criminalizing anything is a political action, and not a scientific achievement. Anslinger did what every successful moral entrepreneur does: he hijacked the empiricists' account of what is and turned it into the moral, political, and ideological equivalent of what should be. Soon the discursive mechanics of criminalization were not only set upon marijuana users, but also African Americans, Hispanics, communists, and even America's poor.

Anslinger also focused on the connection between jazz musicians and marijuana. Through the FBN, he kept files on Jackie Gleason, individuals associated with the NBC orchestra and the Milton Berle Show, and musicians such as Dizzy Gillespie. Some scholars refer to Anslinger's broad anti-marijuana stereotypes as "reefer racism" (Herer, 1985: 76). Nevertheless, reefer racism was not the only unusual artifact of the 1950s revealed by my Archaeology. Another artifact of interest was the Stepping Stone Theory, the precursor for today's Gateway Theory.

The Gateway Theory of the 1980s and 1990s was not an invention of the Just Say No! campaign (associated with Nancy Reagan), but a resurfacing of the Stepping Stone Theory which emerged during the 1950s and in conjunction with the Boggs Act. The Stepping Stone Theory served to de-normalize users in the eyes of a naive American public. Three decades later, America's first official Drug Czar, William Bennett, once again de-normalized marijuana users with the *ad hoc* Gateway Theory. Nevertheless, the Boggs Act Hearings revealed some of the inconsistencies associated with the information delivered to congressional representatives. While Dr. Isbell seemed to be normalizing marijuana users, Anslinger seemed to be denormalizing marijuana users and over time, Anslinger's charismatic leadership seemed to be more persuasive than the findings of Dr. Isbell.

If Anslinger's goal was to de-normalize cannabis users, he was extremely successful. By creating a completely new population of moral deviants and criminals, Anslinger also successfully created the need for a new bureaucracy to be empowered with funding to combat the newly created epidemic of immorality and lawlessness. Anslinger was able to foster budgetary priority for the young law enforcement bureaucracies of drug prohibition while also avoid obstacles to achieving his goals. By achieving these goals, Anslinger's legacy is still very much a part of contemporary America's current system of marijuana prohibition.

Ironically, some of Anslinger's allies in the Boggs Act hearings were the very same addicts that Anslinger had criminalized throughout his career. Some victims of illicit drug abuse agreed with the anti-drug statements made by Anslinger and his colleagues of prohibition. Three former addicts testified in support of the Boggs Act. These reformed addicts enthusiastically helped to popularize the evils of self-destructive and compulsive behavior associated with marijuana use. During these testimonies, all of the witnesses placed a high value on the role of the government to protect its citizens from the merciless influence of marijuana.

In addition to the claims making activities associated with Anslinger and his colleagues, other contingencies were also at play. Contingencies such as the anti-drug and anti-communist campaigns of the late 1940s and early 1950s assured the passage of the Boggs Act. During this period, Americans were fixated by the external threat from communist Russia and by an internal threat of societal instability by way of counterculture drug use. Bonnie and Whitebread (1970) state:

> For example, in 1949 the FBN had begun to encourage the largest cities to form special narcotics squads to deal especially with the drug problem. By 1951, however, only New York and Los Angeles had formed the separate police detail the FBN had requested. Thus even if one were tempted to try to correct for improvements in the law enforcement machinery, the seizure figures for the late 40's and 50's do sustain the notion that the traffic in marijuana increased from 1948

to 1951 . . . As with the hard narcotics, Congress was especially alarmed by the alleged spread of marijuana to white teenagers and school children.

The Boggs Act was a promise to protect the law-abiding citizens of America through introducing draconian penalties for all different types of drug violations (Bonnie and Whitebread, 1970). Under the Boggs Act, for the first time at the federal level, marijuana was included with all of the other narcotics under uniform penalties for drug offenders. Within the context of the Boggs Act, marijuana received the definition and treatment of a narcotic drug.

The Boggs Act hearings rationalized the restrictive treatment of marijuana because marijuana was the stepping stone drug to opiate addiction. Through empowering federal law enforcement bureaucratic machinery, the Boggs Act assisted authorities interested in capturing the evil that walked among all Americans. One example of the many anecdotal stories associated with marijuana-induced evil appears below. Such stories served to justify the existence and proliferation of the newly established federally funded effort to eradicate marijuana. These anecdotal stories served as evidence to substantiate the creation and reproduction of marijuana criminals. The following is a quote from Anslinger and Tompkins' 1953 book, *The Traffic in Narcotics.*

> On a Saturday evening in November, 1945, a pretty seventeen month-old baby girl was left in the family car while her parents went in search of a relative. When they returned to the car less than ten minutes later, the baby had disappeared. The next afternoon, scarcely 200 yards away, the body was found in the furrow of a cotton field. The baby was naked except for one small white shoe and a red-knitted bonnet. She had been violated. Teeth marks covered her body. Her tiny contorted face had been shoved into the mud and particles of dirt in her lungs showed that she had been alive at the time and suffocated later. Police arrested a twenty-five-year-old cotton picker, Paul G., who readily admitted kidnapping the child and "spanking her a little bit." G. stated that on the Saturday evening in question he had been drinking when a friend offered him a reefer which he accepted and smoked. Further intoxicants followed. Then

G. went to a dance hall, from which he departed because no one would dance with him in his condition. As he left, he heard the child crying in a car. Annoyed, he picked up the infant and spanked her, but remembers nothing further except he "guesses he just went crazy." His next recollection was when he came to in his cabin the following morning with mud and blood on his clothes. For what the district attorney described as "the most horrible, the most brutal crime in the history of the area," Paul G. was sentenced to death. The final words of his counsel are well worth remembering: "The real criminal in this case is marihuana!" (Anslinger and Tompkins, 1953: 18-26).

The anecdotes of evil and horror spun by Anslinger and Tompkins were necessary to the processual success of marijuana criminalization. The targeted use of horror stories defined the use of marijuana in conjunction with the corruption of all that is good and moral within our social order. Medical terms no longer expressed marijuana as a medication. In fact, the document itself foils any attempt to justify the use of marijuana as a legitimate medicine by asserting:

In discussing its use, one fact should be emphasized at once. Whereas the opiates can be a blessing when properly used, marihuana has no therapeutic value, and its [marijuana] use is therefore always an abuse and a vice. This important fact should never be forgotten, and pharmacopoeias throughout the world have generally expunged it (Anslinger and Tompkins, 1953: 18-26).

If the key to medicalization is the definitional usage then the key to criminalization is also the definitional usage. By the authority given to these claims makers, the criminalized definition of marijuana allowed the authors of the above quotation to tautologically conclude, "Its use is therefore always an abuse and a vice" (Anslinger and Tompkins, 1953: 18-26).

Sixth Core Legislative Event: The Narcotics Control Act of 1956

In many respects, the Narcotics Control Act of 1956 was an echo of many of the same arguments that buttressed the passage of the Boggs Act. The Narcotics Control Act of 1956 attempted to shore up existing controls of marijuana and narcotic drugs. Penalties for the production and distribution of these substances were increased. Mandatory minimum sentences and fines increased with no distinction between low-level users and high-level traffickers. During this period, Senator Price Daniel (D-TX) received the appointment to chair the Senate Subcommittee, charged with investigating the nation's marijuana problem. The Daniel Subcommittee Hearings emerged as a result.

On February 21, 1955, Senator Price Daniel introduced Senate Resolution 60. By this action, Senator Daniel authorized the formation of a new Senate Judiciary Committee to investigate the relevant issues associated with the debate. Senator Daniel sponsored the resolution and was named chairperson of the Subcommittee hearings, hence the name, Daniel Subcommittee Hearings. A piece of the Daniel Subcommittee transcripts appears below (King, 1972).

> **Senator Butler**. Doctor, is it your testimony that an addict who has a supply of drugs sufficient to keep him from experiencing pain and suffering that he would experience without that drug could be a useful citizen and pursue a normal occupation?
>
> **Dr. Howe**. In a great many instances that is the fact. We see it right now. . . There is evidence in all countries of that, that given a small amount of drugs, enough to prevent withdrawal symptoms, many of these individuals-and there is even further than that, there is medical evidence that suggests that some psychopathic individuals are better off with the drugs than they are when you take them away from them.
>
> **Senator Butler**. Would you say the alcoholic is much more of a potential threat to society than the addict?
>
> **Dr. Howe**. No question about it. That goes without question.
>
> **Senator Daniel**. Well no, Doctor, you might have said something a moment ago that you did not mean exactly as it was said, that the drug addict, when he had his heroin or his morphine, that he then is restored to a normal situation as far as he is concerned, and, therefore, he can go about his business just as anyone else.
>
> **Dr. Howe**. That is right.
>
> **Senator Daniel**. Now, is that an accurate statement?
>
> **Dr. Howe**. That is right . . .
>
> **Senator Daniel**. Which is right, I do not know? I hope we will have enough statistics here to help us clear up the matter. But now, if you have two people with the same mental faculties, one under enough heroin or morphine to take care of his addiction, and the other person

not addicted at all, not under the influence of any type of opiate, what would be his mental faculties as compared with a person, a normal person, without any opiates?
Dr. Howe. Well, he is quiet, he is comfortable, and he wants to be let alone. He will do his job; he has no enemies or anything (King, 1972).

The Daniel Committee Hearings were held in several different locations, including Philadelphia, Los Angeles, San Francisco, Chicago, Detroit, Cleveland, Austin, San Antonio, Fort Worth, Houston, and Dallas. These hearings, held literally throughout the entire country, produced 8,000 pages of official transcripts. The above quote is nothing less than a sliver of text gleaned from the hearings that took place in New York.

In July of 1956, President Eisenhower signed the Narcotic Control Act of 1956 into law. Congress rushed the legislation through most uneventfully. Absent of all questions, advocacies, and dissents that characterized the Daniel Subcommittee Hearings. To restate, in keeping with the tradition of punitive legislative escalation set by the Boggs Act, the Narcotics Control Act of 1956 increased fines and sentences. Here, the death penalty, for cases where heroin was involved, was part of the dialogue. The federal law prohibited the suspending of sentences and the granting of parole, except in the case of a first-time offender guilty of possession only. Most importantly, the federal customs and narcotic agents were empowered to carry weapons, arrest without warrants and even serve warrants. In addition, agents would oversee the deportation of illegal immigrants associated with drug violations. The Daniel Subcommittee Hearings were important not for their high levels of inaccuracies but for their superficial, yet lengthy, examination and thorough dismissal of any solutions, which may have entailed methods associated with "treatment or prevention" (King, 1972).

If H.J. Anslinger had a counterpart, his name was Hubert Howe. Dr. Hubert S. Howe was Henry Ford's personal physician. Additionally, Dr. Howe was a part time claims maker for the medical profession. Eventually, Howe began to aggressively pursue the administrative turf medical practitioners had recently lost to the anti-drug establishment. According to King (1972), Dr. Howe "persuaded the New York Academy of Medicine to adopt reform… [And facilitated a] parade of articles and tracts [which soon] followed." Some of the anti-criminalization titles were:

- Should We Legalize Narcotics?
- We're Bungling the Narcotics Problem
- How Much of a Menace Is the Drug Menace?
- The Dope Addict – Criminal or Patient?
- This Problem of Narcotic Addiction – Let's Face It Sensibly
- Let's Stop This Narcotics Hysteria!

The Daniel Subcommittee transcripts produced a dance of sorts between the rationale of Dr. Howe and the rationale of Senator Daniel. Dr. Howe asserted that some addicts, given a steady supply of narcotics, may very well be more productive workers than had they been given no access to medication. The doctor went on to state that some psychopathic individuals function more appropriately while they are addicted and medicating themselves with narcotics. Some addicts, he asserted, may even function at a higher level than some individuals that are compulsively medicating themselves with alcohol (i.e., alcoholics). Another exchange takes place wherein Senator Daniel asked for the use of statistics to help clear up the issue under debate. Unlike Howe, H. J. Anslinger easily provided statements for the senators containing statistics. Whether or not Anslinger's statistics were valid or reliable does not matter to my investigation.

> **Anslinger.** Now, as to the question of crime, in Formosa, the only place where they actually made a study, Dr. Tu of the University of Taipei made this study, and he showed that criminality – of the crimes committed in Formosa at the time these monopolies or the legalized sale of drugs were in effect, 70 per cent of the crimes were committed by opium smokers who got their narcotics at Government shops at very cheap prices a few cents a day; whereas only 30 per cent of the crimes that were committed were committed by non-smokers. Now, these proponents just skirt this question of opium

smoking . . . Now, they also brush marijuana and cocaine aside . . .
I do not know what they say, they just say nothing about marijuana
or how it is to be handled; they just avoid that (King, 1972).

Anslinger turned complex social phenomena into easy to understand math (i.e.,
descriptive statistics). This permitted Anslinger's argument to prevail. Since the
medical experts failed to deliver a simple and concise argument for the senators to
understand, their knowledge about the complexity of the problem at hand was no
longer under serious consideration.

The medical experts received admonishment for their failure to marshal the
simple descriptive statistics, which could sum up their position. Senator Daniel
stated, "I will say to you frankly, Doctor [Howe], that I am disappointed that this
group, after all the years of work and study with drug addicts, does not have a more
definite position" (King, 1972). Senator Daniel echoed contemporary frustration
among politicians and policy makers advocating the use of medicalization as a
primary engine for controlling substance abuse in society. Conversely, Anslinger,
by 1956, had spent many hours testifying in Congressional hearings. He knew how
to simplify complex information. He knew his credentials (as a fellow member of
the beltway bureaucratic oligarchy) were enough to carry his stories and swathe them
in constructions of legitimacy and truth.

If Dr. Howe was resting on the laurels of sovereignty associated with the
scientific method, he did not prepare for Anslinger's well-oiled engine of moral
entrepreneurialism. The sophisticated discursive machinery of medicalization was
virtually incomprehensible to Senator Daniel. He was, however, intimate with the
easy to understand discursive machinery of criminalization. In a bizarre exchange,
Senator Daniel begins, over the course of the hearings, to refer to H. J. Anslinger as
"Doctor" Anslinger. Somehow, Senator Daniel's awareness of the fact that H. J.
Anslinger was, in the past, awarded an "obscure honorary degree" (King, 1972). In
this regard, Senator Daniel may have attempted to privilege and legitimize
Anslinger's discourse of criminalization (which Senator Daniel understood and

spoke semi-fluently) by referring to Anslinger as Doctor. While the following two quotations serve to illustrate these two different complexes of knowledge, they also serve to summarize, in part, the two positions of the debate in an economic fashion:

Dr. Howe. Many people recoil with horror at the suggestion of furnishing low-cost drugs to addicts, even under the best system of supervision which our Government can devise. For those of us who want to pass laws prohibiting everything undesirable and many Americans seem to, it is a thoroughly startling idea. The public has yet to grasp the fact that addicts are dangerous when they are without their drugs, not when they are with them. They do not realize that in Britain this problem has been solved. The question, therefore, clearly is: Why should we have narcotic laws, the practical effect of which is to force people to rob, steal, proselyte, and prostitute, in order to support their habit, especially when the need for criminal activity can be prevented for a few cents worth of drugs per addict, per day? . . . One may also consider that, after 40 years of the Harrison Act, the addict still obtains his drug, unless he is in the strictest form of incarceration. We are not saying to give the addicts more drugs. We are simply advising a different method of distribution. The Government says he cannot get it legally; therefore, he has got to steal and rob, and so on, in order to get it. Well, he gets it, but we believe there is a better method of distribution than that. We are not in any way advocating that they get more than they need. But every addict gets his drug right now. As I say, unless he is in jail, every addict gets his drug and many of them get it in jail, at least they do in New York. Why not let him have his minimum requirement under licensed medical supervision, rather than force him to get it by criminal activities, through criminal channels? We now have, in the narcotic black market, a matchless machine for the manufacture of criminals. Isn't it about time we looked over the horizon to see how the problem has been solved elsewhere?
Senator Daniel. Gentlemen, I tell you that, after sitting through two more days of hearings here, I am convinced that we are never going to lick this problem of the drug traffic until we get the addicts off the streets of this country. They have got to be taken off the streets, and I know it is hard. Some of the enforcement officers think it is best to get them in the jails temporarily, and the different States have passed those kinds of laws. I would like to see us at the same time that we set up our laws to take them off the streets, set up some place to have them go and get a chance for treatment, and then if they won't take it, and you cannot do anything with them, then, it seems to me, it is

just as humane to put them in some kind of a colony or some kind of farm or institution like you do mental patients...Any other comments, gentlemen? I think you see that what this Committee is driving at and what kind of information we would like to have now... (King, 1972).

Both positions eventually find compromise. Anslinger, as quoted below, illustrates the compromise whereby these very different complexes of knowledge and disciplinary forms of power cohabit within the architecture of state sponsored physical and mental coercion. Anslinger's brainchild exemplifies the way by which power and knowledge work together through a tapestry of language, chemical enhancement and physical restraint. Anslinger bookends Senator Daniel's lead in the following:

> **Mr. Anslinger**. Yes, sir. The legalized-you have to get an addict under legal restraint. We have got to have a system of compulsory hospitalization. That is my recommendation on how to treat the addicts. I do not think any other system-any other system is doomed to failure...
> **Senator Daniel**. You think compulsory commitment and treatment is the only solution?
> **Mr. Anslinger**. That is what I have felt, and I think you will find that the experts on the United Nations' Narcotic Commission are in accord, that you must have hospitalization, compulsory hospitalization. That is the opinion of the Germans, the French; and nearly all the European countries feel that way (King, 1972).

The economical nature of Anslinger's suggestion presented to the subcommittee a merger between the therapeutic and paternalistic powers. Even though Anslinger was not exclusively talking about marijuana users as addicts in the quote above, it appears that the only substantive issue that both parties agreed on was the inability of adults to act responsibly with their freedoms and liberties, as afforded to them under their own Constitution and Bill of Rights. Whether or not the gaze of institutional watch should be levied against the infantilized citizenry never made it onto the table.

Anslinger, Howe, and Daniel efficiently engaged in devising a machine to dole out subjectivity. The transcripts reveal the blueprints of a machine of social control. There was no discussion of whether or not their proposed machinery stood on solid Constitutional ground and, as a result, the most imperative and vital debate never took place. The issue of Constitutional viability, through neglect, became a non-issue.

Seventh Core Legislative Event: The Controlled Substance Act of 1970

The Controlled Substance Act of 1970 (CSA) was implemented by the Bureau of Narcotics and Dangerous Drugs (BNDD) in the early 1970s and is still enforced today, in variant form, by the nation's contemporary administration for enforcing drug laws, the Drug Enforcement Agency (DEA). The CSA of 1970 is of particular interest to my Archaeology due to the mere fact that the Act merged more than fifty separate portions of existing and fragmented drug laws. The Act was an effective and efficient law that brought about the consolidation of many different federal drug policies into one coherent document. As a result, United States history was forever changed. The law came with rules and regulations that illustrated the classification process for problematic substances. These new drug classifications were eventually implemented into the ongoing subjectivity of all those targeted by the anti-drug war engine (DEA, 2004).

> This law brings together a number of laws regulating the manufacture and distribution of narcotics, stimulants, depressants, hallucinogens, anabolic steroids, and chemicals used in the illicit production of controlled substances. All substances are placed in one of five schedules, based on medicinal value, harmfulness, and potential for abuse or addiction, with Schedule I reserved for the most dangerous drugs that have no recognized medical use.

Most notably, the Controlled Substance Act of 1970 brought into existence Schedules I-V (since altered several times), and for all intents and purposes established the scaffold of legislative authority that today's DEA still enjoys. The drugs of interest were defined, categorized, and placed into schedules based upon three criteria: "how dangerous they are, their potential for abuse and addiction, and whether they possess legitimate medical value" (DEA, 2004).

The Controlled Substance Act of 1970 is a piece of legislation that exemplifies what philosopher Jeffrey Reiman refers to as "historical inertia" (Reiman, 2004: 64-65, 159-160). By this, he means the way by which "policies came to be what they are" and how these policies "persist in the face of their failure to achieve either security or justice" (Reiman, 2004: 159-160). To illustrate, I quote a document from the Bureau of Narcotics and Dangerous Drugs (BNDD) issued during "Drug Education Week in 1970" from President Nixon (DEA, 2004).

> The past decade has seen the abuse of drugs grow from essentially a local police problem into a serious threat to the health and safety of millions of Americans. The number of narcotics addicts in the United States is estimated to be in the hundreds of thousands and the effects of their addiction spread far beyond their own lives. Statistics tell but a part of the tragedy of drug abuse. The crippled lives of young Americans, the shattered hopes of their parents, the rending of the social fabric – as addicts inevitably turn to crime in order to supply a costly habit – these are the personal tragedies, the human disasters that tell the real story of what drug abuse does to individuals and can do to our nation.

Nixon's memo, Proclamation 3981, declared the existence of an annual official Drug Education Week to take place sometime in May and declared an unofficial war against drugs. His memo called upon the Federal Government, Departments of Justice, Health, Education, and Welfare, educators, administrators of the academic community, state and local governments, businesses, professionals, civil groups, media, clergy, and all other persons who interact with young Americans, to battle an abstract enemy by waging an abstract war. The passage of the Controlled Substance Act (CSA) of 1970 followed the Presidential BNDD Bulletin (DEA, 2004).

Upon passing the 1970 Act, Congress concluded that they needed more information to assess the uses and abuses associated with marijuana. Congress even went so far as to ask for the establishment of a special Presidential Commission to produce a comprehensive assessment. President Nixon established this commission in 1971. The Shafer Commission, also called the National Commission on Marijuana and Drug Abuse, issued its final report in March of 1972 entitled, "Marihuana: A Signal of Misunderstanding" and was the most definitive look at marijuana that the U.S. Government had ever produced (CSDP, 2002).

The Shafer Commission issued recommendations that flew in the face of Nixon's private views about the proper handling/prohibition of marijuana. President Nixon reportedly said, "We need, and I use the word 'all-out war,' on all fronts . . . have to attack on all fronts," to House Representative "Bob" Haldeman on the day before the Shafer Commission released its findings and summarily recommended decriminalization for offenses involving marijuana possession. The Shafer Commission, however, went so far as to recommend no criminal or civil penalties under state or federal laws (CSDP, 2002). Even so, the results of the Shafer report fell upon deaf ears. As a result, America soon began escalating Nixon's all out war on drugs, and the citizens who used them. To accomplish his aims, Nixon created a super agency to oversee drug prohibition in America and the DEA was born.

The DEA's on-line history of itself includes the surface rationale for creating the agency in the first place. Among other reasons, President Nixon and Congress felt the need to establish a "superagency to provide the momentum needed to coordinate all federal efforts related to drug enforcement outside the Justice Department, especially the gathering of intelligence . . .," so as to put "an end to the interagency rivalries that have undermined federal drug law enforcement, especially the rivalry between the BNDD and the U.S. Customs Service" (DEA, 2004).

The Nixon Administration and Congress did in fact provide the super-agency with momentum and bureaucratic inertia (ONDCP, 2002: 6). To illustrate how much the DEA has grown, I briefly examine the humble beginnings of a super-agency in its infancy. For example, in 1972, the agency employed 2,775 individuals and in 2005, the agency employed 10,894. In 1972, the budget for the entire DEA was 65.2 million. In 2005, the budget of the DEA was 2.141 billion dollars (U.S. Dept. of

Justice, 2005). In short, the DEA's rate of growth over three decades, with respect to budgetary and personnel matters, was remarkable.

Eighth Core Legislative Event: Comprehensive Crime Control of 1984

The administration of punishment for lawbreakers under Reagan was a black and white issue (literally and figuratively), to set an anti-marijuana agenda that was supposed to be easy to understand and implement. The proposed solution was simple: punish swiftly and punish harshly. Before these political, moral, and ideological shifts in policy could take place in totality, a new language under Reagan had to replace the old language of public health and public welfare that was associated with the Carter Administration. Exhumed was Anslinger's Stepping Stone Theory along with a brand new form of McCarthyism to rout out internal and external threats to the social moral order.

As America's military industrial complex was empowered through budgetary primacy, anti-communist rhetoric escalated. Counterculture politicos, "uppity" minority members, and the economically disadvantaged were on the other end of a new tough on crime/law and order approach, which empowered the internal arm of national defense (i.e., the correctional industrial complex). The Reagan Administration sought to bring the moral majority back into the Garden of Eden, or at least back into the 1950s, where America could be drug free, patriarchal, and innocent once again.

The proverbial tree of knowledge had introduced evil into the heart of America, and drug policy reform in America became a key issue under Reagan's leadership. The language (or truth) of the Carter Administration's drug policies may have been the first casualty of Reagan's new drug policy initiatives. Baum (1996) illustrates Reagan's anti-drug discourse as closed and free from academic inquiry or debate, ensuring its success.

> Dependent as it was on presenting marijuana as Public Drug Enemy
> Number One, Reagan's War on Drugs couldn't withstand scientific
> debate. Placed against heroin – or for that matter alcohol, tobacco,
> poor prenatal care, workplace accidents, and a myriad of other public

> health problems – marijuana pales by comparison. So rather than invite opponents onto the playing fields of science and data, [those who worked for the Reagan Administration] attempted to ban the game altogether (Baum, 1996: 164).

The National Institute on Drug Abuse, or NIDA, was at the time and still is the leading national organization that studies the science of drug abuse and addiction. The director of NIDA during the early years of the Reagan administration was William Pollin. According to Baum (1996: 164), under Pollin's instruction, all NIDA publications having to do with drug treatment, prevention, and abuse were required to undergo review. Any NIDA publications containing the word "social" received a tag for removal from circulation. Pollin issued an official request to librarians to purge all materials listed by NIDA as suspect. Pollin requested, "These publications reflect preliminary marijuana and cocaine research findings that often found equivocal results. I strongly suggest that you purge your collection of these old materials" (Baum, 1996: 164). Sixty-four NIDA booklets were on the list. Among them, all published between 1975 through 1979, were the following titles:

- Drug Abuse Films: Multicultural Film Catalog
- Can Drug Abuse Be Prevented in the Black Community?
- Multicultural Perspectives in Drug Abuse: An Annotated Guide to the Literature
- The Rap Kit: Resources for Alternative Pursuits
- A Woman's Choice: Deciding about Drugs

To control language is to control knowledge. As mentioned before, knowledge receives its employment from power.

Power and knowledge are allied and work together through language. If there are no words for "it," then "it" does not exist. If power instructs knowledge to do work, the work is undertaken. If power instructs knowledge not to work, then the work is not undertaken. If power instructs knowledge to erase work completed in conflict of existing power, then knowledge destroys any adversarial information incongruent with current power. History undergoes repeated revisions to be in harmony with contemporary forms of power. As contemporary forms of power change in character, history must also change. In turn, knowledge, which is determined by power to be at odds or dissimilar with contemporary forms of power, receives labels of abnormal, illegitimate, useless, and even bad or immoral. No power literally means no truth and no knowledge.

Academic researchers who studied illicit drug policy and produced knowledge about illicit drug use in America during the 1970's were not the only threats to Reagan's Administration. The medical industrial complex was also standing in the way of the criminal justice industry acquiring some of the bureaucratic administrative turf that it now possesses. While Ph.D.s who depended upon large governmental grants were easily controlled through restricting funding, the authority that doctors held over their patients was more difficult for criminal justice bureaucracies to annex.

In a document published by the U.S. Government entitled "Legislative History of Federal Drug Law Supports Authority to Act Against Physician-Assisted Suicide," a story emerges wherein the Comprehensive Crime Control of 1984 allowed the DEA to commandeer what little authority remained for physicians to treat seriously ill patients in a manner that was considerably autonomous. The document attempts to confront and correct any misunderstanding as to the authority of the federal government to use federal law to prosecute physicians who inappropriately prescribe controlled and scheduled medications.

It is important to understand that the prime intent of the 1984 law was not to battle illicit street drugs such as marijuana or heroin. Rather, the law's prime intent was to empower DEA officials to regulate medically legitimate drugs that were being diverted or misused for illegitimate purposes. Assisted suicide by a licensed physician was among the illegitimate uses of these federally regulated substances. The rationale for needing the law to police licensed physicians, legal drug manufactures, and law-abiding pharmacists is in the Congressional Record. Some of the more emphatic statements associated with the passage of the legislation are quoted below.

> **Rep. Hughes.** [The problem had]...failed to get the societal or the enforcement attention that it deserves...The bill gives to DEA greater latitude to suspend or revoke the registration of a practitioner who dispenses drugs in a manner that threatens the public health and safety...prescription drugs are responsible for close to 70 percent of the deaths and injuries due to drug abuse (Cong. Record, 9/18/84, H9679).
> **Rep. Waxman.** Today's pusher is not always a back alley salesman. He or she may well be a highly educated health professional... Drugs legally manufactured for use in medicine are responsible for a substantial majority of drug-related deaths and injuries (Hearing of July 31, 1984, Hearing Record No. 98-168, p. 365).

The DEA took power away from the medical industrial complex, in large part because the AMA failed to lobby around their special interests and preserve their own administrative and bureaucratic turf. Once again, knowledge serves power and knowledge is active in play when knowledge suits the interests of power. The selective use of knowledge by power is not a conspiracy; it is the basis of our academic order.

Ninth Core Legislative Event: The Anti Drug Abuse Act of 1986

The drug war seemed to go nuclear in 1986 with the passage of the Anti Drug Abuse Act. A key event often mentioned as a precipitating moment or catalyst for the passage of the 1986 Act was the death of a promising young basketball star, Len Bias. Bias was an athlete from University of Maryland and a second-round draft pick who landed a contract with the Boston Celtics. On June 19, 1986, Bias tragically died of a heart seizure (Goode, 2005: 110). The police issued a statement that indicated Bias was celebrating with friends over the lucrative professional basketball contract he just signed. While Bias reportedly ingested excessive amounts of alcohol that night, the press ran with the fact that he had also used cocaine. Downplayed was the fact that he had snorted powder cocaine and given was the impression, to the public through sensational media attention, that crack cocaine was the specific substance responsible for the death. The press gave very little discussion to the fact that, willingly and foolishly, Bias chose to ingest and mix irresponsible amounts of alcohol and cocaine. If Bias did make a choice, his choice was framed within the spatial and temporal location of his death. For example, the press painted a picture of a talented young man who regretfully chose to get high on cocaine while simultaneously rejecting one of capitalist America's cherished achievements: to become extremely wealthy. To understand the surfaces of emergence by which the death of Bias became understandable to the public, puts the incident into proper perspective. The death of Bias was a catalyst to the passage of The Anti Drug Abuse Act of 1986 as well as an important contingency in escalating America's war against marijuana.

The death of Bias was a catalytic event and the event occurred under President Reagan's watch. Ronald Reagan was quite possibly the most anti-drug president that America has ever had. Picking up where Nixon left off, Reagan's anti-communist and anti-crime agenda swept the nation. However, in the beginning of the Reagan Era, Nancy Reagan was in trouble, with a poor relationship with the media. The press had effectively painted a picture of the First Lady as excessive and extravagant. The American Press referred to her as a Queen rather than a First Lady. Goode elaborates:

> Shortly after. . . Nancy Reagan, the First Lady attended the wedding of Prince Charles and Lady Diana. Traveling with "four boxes, twenty dresses, a hair dresser, a photographer, sixteen security agents, [and two] chaperones," the trip "had been a public relations disaster." The press attacked her extravagance . . . on the same day that she ordered $200,000 worth of china for the White House table, the Agriculture Department announced that for the purposes of government-supported lunches for the poor, catsup would be classified as a vegetable . . . Mrs. Reagan was in hot public relations water. (Goode, 2005: 110)

To counteract her poor public image, the First Lady's Just Say No! anti-drug, pro-parent campaign came at the perfect time. The First Lady's anti-drug and pro-parent campaign was the perfect cause to adopt. It was uncontroversial to be in favor of parenting, and no one wanted their child to break the law by abusing illicit drugs. By 1985, her public relations machine had given birth to the Just Say No anti-drug campaign to educate American children about the evils of illegal drugs. Just Say No! was the catch phrase of the Reagan/Bush years. It was the sound bite that the drug war needed. Once the statement had emerged to the surface of historical specificity, the statement began to reproduce at an exponential rate.

Most importantly, Just Say No effectively shut out any discursive challenge to the tough on crime and crime as drugs law and order campaign associated with the Reagan presidency. Under Reagan, the decriminalization of marijuana was no longer on the table for discussion. There was no need to conduct research on the therapeutic value of marijuana. There was no need to debate decriminalization. To reduce the entire debate to one word: No! was a brilliant public policy *coup d'état*. The anti-drug discursive coercive machinery was officially closed for the next decade. The anti-drug discourse became and remained sovereign until 1996.

Nevertheless, the *Just Say No* campaign was not the only surface on which the death of Bias emerged. On November 29, 1985, the year before Bias' death, the New York Times ran a story calling attention to a new form of cocaine causing a moral panic on the inner city streets of America's largest city. The new form of cocaine was said to be more concentrated, easy to make, and cheap to buy and smoke. The high was brief but intense. Those who used the drug underwent a powerful psychologically reinforcing experience whereby the user, over time, had his or her sense of morality fragmented. The name of the drug was crack, for the fact that when the user put the drug to flame the white powered rock made a popping, cracking, or snapping sound. Drugs, or all illicit drugs, became the target for de-normalization in the brilliant yet infantile *Just Say No* public relations campaign.

The Just Say No campaign, the budding crack epidemic of immorality, and the law and order Reagan Administration were not the only contingencies at play. In addition, there was a legislative body of Democrats looking to shed their ties to a very unpopular former President, Jimmy Carter. During the 1984 election, the general impression was that the Republicans had successfully out-flanked the Democrats by asserting that the Democrats were soft on crime. The death of Bias took place just before the July 4 congressional recess. During the break, the Speaker of the House heard from his constituency that drugs were the problem. It was drugs that stopped the Celtics from gaining Len Bias, their second round draft pick. Drugs were the issue by which the Democrats could show the country that they, too, were harsh on crime, criminals, and immorality. They, too, could use the law to protect the poor from the evils of drugs. If need be, they too, could incarcerate their way out of the moral panic that had emerged. After the death of Bias, drugs were cast as the number one threat to the health and well-being of the nation. There was great political potential in sponsoring a successful anti-drug bill, and the Democrats did manage to appear tough but not intelligent. The bill passed and was law within four months, a breakneck pace by any standard (Bikel, 1999).

The war on drugs seemed to explode into the news again in 1988 when Congress passed another pre-November Anti-Drug Law. The 1988 Anti-Drug legislation, in part, empowered prosecutors to make everyone involved in a drug conspiracy liable for every act of the drug conspiracy. Under federal law, if a college student ended up introducing two people who began dealing in marijuana later, the said college student became liable for all of the marijuana the two people ever grew or distributed together. Under federal law a watchman of a grow room became not only responsible for all marijuana sold from the said grow room, but s/he also became legally culpable for all of the marijuana which was ever grown and sold by all of the members of the marijuana conspiracy. The Anti-Drug legislation of 1988 resulted in a significant increase in the prison population. "Within six years, the number of drug cases in federal prisons increased by 300 percent. From 1986 to 1998 it was up by 450 percent" (Bikel, 1999). In 2004 alone, America arrested over 700,000 individuals on marijuana charges; most for possession.

Conclusions from the Archaeology of Marijuana Criminalization

In this chapter, I illustrated the life course of a deviant designation through the study of the process of marijuana criminalization. Before 1906, the deviant status of the medicinal marijuana user (i.e., the sick) existed before marijuana use became a criminal action. Therefore, my Archaeology began at the end of the pre-criminalization era (1906). The years prior to 1906 did not undergo examination due to a lack of time and resources. I assumed that the use of medicinal marijuana before 1906 was abnormal, yet a legitimate herbal remedy. While marijuana use in 1906 was not immoral, it was deviant and not the norm. Those who smoked marijuana in 1906 and prior for medical purposes were abnormal or deviant but not criminal.

The Archaeology has illustrated the way by which marijuana, as a legitimate herbal remedy, has become redefined over time, from a harmless deviant behavior into a harmful, criminal behavior. Because of this, several legislative Acts underwent examination by my Archaeology. In so doing, I illustrated their significance to an overall understanding of how marijuana became a criminal action, by the federal government during the 1900s. These Acts from 1906 to 1986 (and 1988) provided a temporal order by which statements from the archive satellite around. I pulled numerous statements from the archive and examined data associated with historically specific core legislative events. These events and their associate data underwent examination to illustrate the process of marijuana criminalization throughout the 1900s. Even so, these core federal legislative Acts were not the only contingencies at play throughout the historically specific process of marijuana criminalization.

Throughout this chapter, I argued that the process of marijuana criminalization facilitated (and was facilitated by) numerous contingencies, one being the end of alcohol prohibition. The federal machinery of alcohol prohibition had been established to carry out a constitutional mandate and it possessed powerful political, fiscal, and bureaucratic inertia. This inertia was then directed away from alcohol prohibition and toward a new form of prohibition (i.e., marijuana prohibition). In this regard, marijuana prohibition legislation evaded the attention of the middle class who, by then, had become suspicious of alcohol prohibition.

In addition, I argued that during this period, the Supreme Court's decision to affirm the constitutionality of the federal government to levy a prohibitory tax on Americans was another important contingency (See above discussion entitled "Fourth Core Legislative Event-The Marijuana Tax Act of 1937"). The prohibition of marijuana was, in part, the product of a prohibitory tax specifically designed and implemented (not to exclusively generate revenue for the federal government) to discourage the citizenry of America from using marijuana recreationally and/or medicinally. I argued that the process of marijuana criminalization could not have emerged under a different set of temporal and spatial contingencies.

In this chapter, I illustrated obvious and ignored ways by which power and knowledge work together through language and become allied. Throughout my analysis, I demonstrated that power employs "knowledge" only when a particular truth brand serves to benefit the powerful. If information or knowledge produced specific brands of truth that challenged or threatened existing systems of power, power did not employ knowledge. Through ignoring specific forms of information that challenge the status quo or the powerful, power neutralized adverse forms of information or aggressively destroyed brands of truth, which threatened existing forms of power and sovereign entities of discourse. For example, during the early and mid 1900s, racism against Mexican-Americans and African-Americans was a very real contingency at play that affected the successful nature of marijuana criminalization. However, I argue that racism against Mexican-Americans and African-Americans by Caucasians engaging in cultural protectionism was not a "primary" causal force associated with criminalizing marijuana in the United States. Racism, although very real, did not cause the criminalization. Racism against Mexican-Americans was one of many different contingencies, which taken all together, contributed to the historically specific accident of marijuana criminalization.

In addition, anti-marijuana horror stories were palatable forms of information (or misinformation) for newly developed and newly developing complexes of "knowledge" associated with a rapidly growing system of federal law enforcement. The abstract machinery of marijuana prohibition was easily employed by federal and state governments to protect their power from what they believed to be the dangerous classes (i.e., youth, minorities, and the poor). At the same time, the capitalist elite, or those with a large amount of political, social, and fiscal capital, were allowed to purchase their civil liberties, due process, and other forms of protection from federal and state interference, oversight and/or prosecution. To restate, the wealthy were protected from the government and the government was protected from the poor in part through the mechanism of marijuana prohibition.

Most importantly, my unique contribution to what we currently know about the history of U.S. drug policy is accentuated by my effort to discuss the process of deviant designation change. By doing so, my research puts forth a template by which most deviant designations may be studied as they systematically and uniformly change throughout their life course. I argue that many new deviant designations emerge in the same manner. In addition, I argue that many deviant designations maturate in a similar manner, and prosper under uniform and specific conditions. Lastly, I argue that under specific and rare conditions, semi-permanent deviant designations may enter into hyperactive forms of productivity, ultimately resulting in their own destruction under rare but uniform conditions. The result is that as one deviant designation potentially becomes over-produced and eventually destroyed, another deviant designation is often born. Put another way, the extremes of marijuana criminalization (of yesterday) set the stage for today's highly successful medicinal marijuana campaigns.

Chapter Five

A Genealogy of Marijuana Medicalization

This chapter employs the Foucaultian Method's analytical tool of choice, the Genealogy. The Genealogy is the methodological device that I use to conduct a history of the present effort to medicalize marijuana. Another way to define the Genealogy is to compare and contrast it to its predecessor, the Archaeology. Foucault (1980: 85) does so below, as he differentiates between the methods of Archaeology and Genealogy:

> If we were to characterize it in two terms, then 'Archaeology' would be the appropriate methodology of this analysis of local discursivities, and 'Genealogy' would be the tactics whereby, on the basis of the descriptions of these local discursivities, the subjected knowledges which were thus released would be brought into play.

While Foucaultian terminology can sometimes resemble awkward jargon, the above quote from Foucault is understandable once it has been unpacked (i.e., expanded upon and translated).

Within the context of our research, Foucault's sentence indicates that the Genealogy is a research method that uncovers the tactics of various claims makers. They make use of these tactics to introduce the medical marijuana social movement to the American mainstream. Once introduced, the claims makers use these tactics to lobby for the success of the new social movement. Such tactics may ultimately change the way that the law behaves toward marijuana as well as the people who use the plant for one reason or another.

Studying these tactics is important because these tactics involve changing the way that people talk, think and act toward marijuana today, as well as how people

93

may talk, think, or act toward one another tomorrow. Ultimately, this chapter investigates these tactics and some of their outcomes. In this manner, information about medical marijuana and the mechanisms that release such information to the public undergoes analysis in this chapter's Genealogy. This chapter also demonstrates that these tactics serve to fuel the political success of today's medical marijuana social movement. However, and more importantly, these tactics influence what Americans officially know about marijuana, as well as those using the drug. Importantly, what citizens officially know about marijuana has both intended and unintended public policy consequences. With hundreds of thousands of Americans arrested on marijuana charges in 2004 alone, large numbers of Americans currently experience consequences. As Americans renegotiate their official responses to marijuana, the political and social leaders who are defining the parameters of such a hot button topic debate impact all Americans by using specific tactics to win the debate.

I also examine the tactics used to fuel the production of widely distributed pro-medical marijuana research brands of truth. For example, moral entrepreneurs use research results containing politically favorable outcomes, while ignoring the information that may hinder their political goals and objectives. Outcomes of such selective observation usually support and justify the need to medicalize marijuana as well as the need to decriminalize marijuana for all adult citizens.

Additionally, this chapter examines some of the intended as well as the unintended consequences of marijuana medicalization. As a result, I uncover the unpleasant and unpalatable origins of marijuana medicalization (Kendall and Wickham, 2000: 29). As a method, the Genealogy does not intend to be judgmental. Nevertheless, this chapter's Genealogy intends to be a candid summary of uncomfortable and obvious observations made in the presence of an extremely polarized political pitch (Kendall and Wickham, 2000: 29).

Ultimately, this chapter seeks to allow me, as a researcher, to participate within our present system of thought, to take accountability or ownership for bettering our own and consequently each other's understanding of a misunderstood plant (Kendall and Wickham, 2000: 30). To achieve this, the Foucaultian objective to carry out work "by ourselves upon ourselves as free beings" is pursued (Foucault, 1984: 47). As the Foucaultian Method instructs, "This aspect of Genealogy is thus not so much about knowledge as about 'an agitation from within' toward the capacity for self-reinvention" (Kendall and Wickham, 2000: 30).

As I previously mentioned, Genealogy is simply the application of Archaeology as a methodological device to expose the omnibus discourse of the here and now. Be it criminalization or medicalization, there is an unending quality to coercive discursive entities and the subjects who willingly or unwillingly submit to their influences. Ironically, specific subjects (including social scientists) who exist within specific discursive entities are not likely to reflect upon the totalizing affects of the discursive impulses that can dramatically alter their lives. Genealogy is a strategy for allowing the sociologist/criminologist to make important and overlooked observations. This is an accomplishment, for researchers, made possible by the Genealogy's mandate to break from the totalizing influence of the here and now (Kendall and Wickham, 2000: 30). By employing the analytical device properly, this chapter results in an accurate yet simplistic demystification of the present. In practicing the method, I begin to demystify the present through the descriptions of statements and visibilities. I intend to draw attention to ignored and/or accepted assumptions, currently hidden in plain sight.

Genealogy and the Process of Marijuana Medicalization

In this chapter, Genealogy is the tool that uses an analysis of contemporary statements that describe the ongoing process of medicalization. By using this tool, I create a proverbial motion picture about the medicalization of marijuana as it appears in the present. While the Archaeology's intention, presented in the previous chapter, was to be something of an album of photographic images that recalled the past historical process of marijuana criminalization, the Genealogy sheds light on the liaisons between objects of fiscal power and objects of political power. These objects, and the statements which satellite around them, do not receive descriptions or labels of truth within this chapter. Statements are artifacts of the apparatus of medicalization, nothing more and nothing less. As a result, I employ a problem-based approach while conducting a general history of today's medical marijuana movement.

Through the surface level description of statements, I highlight relationships of power, and the introduction of power occurs throughout this chapter (Kendall and Wickham, 2000: 29). I argue that the key to conducting the Genealogy is to make uncomfortable existing studies of our object of interest. By doing this, I draw attention to the obvious yet actively ignored. Additionally, this chapter introduces the popularized and contemporary representation of the new boss (i.e., medicalization) as nothing more than the old boss (i.e., criminalization), with the new boss displaying an impressive appetite for seizing more and more administrative turf over time. As a result, the Genealogy displays medicalization, like criminalization, as an emergent form of social control.

Through documenting a slow, but dramatic shift in the way that Americans, as a people, have thought about marijuana, I document a shift away from an expensive brand of hard power (i.e., criminalization) toward an economical soft form of power (i.e., medicalization). Therefore, the analysis emphasizes the way by which unpalatable regressions in civil rights continue to be re-packaged and redefined for the public as official public policy progression (i.e., marijuana medicalization).

To illustrate the way by which citizens become and remain docile under medicalization, this chapter illustrates some of what is being hidden (albeit in plain sight) by a most recent discursive system (i.e., medicalization). While the discourse of marijuana criminalization has been, until recently, unopened and rarely challenged by scholarly examinations, I argue that the contemporary process of marijuana medicalization is aggressively discrediting the older discursive machinery of marijuana criminalization.

In sum, this chapter demonstrates that the debate over medicinal marijuana has become increasingly less rational. However, before the abstract machinery of marijuana medicalization can undergo disassembly and specification, I must first marshal evidence of the emergence and proliferation of medical marijuana ballot initiatives. To this aim, I bring into sight a brief summary of the first nine state laws that serve as powerful indicators that medicalization is becoming increasingly popular. As a result, what we as Americans know about marijuana today is dramatically and rapidly undergoing transformation.

Medical Marijuana State Laws: The First Nine
California in 1996

On November 1996, California's voters approved Proposition 215 (Pollan, 1997). The passage of California's Proposition 215 shocked a nation, indoctrinated with the seemingly sovereign discourse of zero-tolerance marijuana prohibition. The New York Times reported, "The passage of Proposition 215 marks the end of 'Just say no' – and the beginning of Americans saying a great many other things about drugs. It is a conversation that the war on drugs may not survive" (Pollan, 1997). In sum, this proposition removed state level criminal penalties for medicinal marijuana patients who possessed a physician's written or oral recommendation for marijuana who resided in the state of California. Under a physician's recommendation, a medical marijuana patient can avoid prosecution by the state of California for using, possessing or even cultivating cannabis.

The passage of the proposition initially set no limits on the amount of cannabis a medicinal marijuana patient could cultivate or possess. Importantly, the new law did not specify which diseases would be eligible for treatment by medicinal marijuana. At first, the state law seemed overly vague, deeming medical marijuana appropriate for any condition, as long as a licensed physician recommended the drug. Nevertheless, two years after the passage of Proposition 215, the New York Times would report, "Defying federal officials, and often state legislators, voters approved initiatives on Tuesday to legalize the medical use of marijuana in Alaska, Arizona, Nevada, Oregon and Washington State" (Brooke, 1998).

Washington, Oregon, and Alaska in 1998

The voters of Washington State approved Measure 692 in November 1998 (Brooke, 1998). Like the California law, Washington's medical marijuana law removed criminal penalties, at the state level, for users of medicinal marijuana. A Professor of Policy Studies at UCLA, Mark Kleiman stated, "I don't think any of these propositions would have passed five years ago...It is no longer possible to buffalo the American people by screaming drugs and having them run away" (Brooke, 1998).

Professor Kleiman was not the only academic engaging in social activism. Ethan Nadelmann, once a professor at Princeton University, was the director of a drug policy institute in New York called the Lindesmith Center. The center was named after Professor Lindesmith who had made a career of challenging H.J. Anslinger and the drug control establishment while it was still in its infancy. As an aside, Anslinger's attack on Professor Lindesmith and Indiana University, for publishing Lindesmith's research, led to President Kennedy's dismissal of Anslinger. Ironically, it would be Lindesmith's name that would pop up again in 1998, as America's drug control establishment would try to, once more, withstand attack.

The Lindesmith Center was among a handful of anti-drug war nonprofit organizations that had received five million dollars to advertise and fund all five of the successful medical marijuana state ballot initiatives (Brooke, 1998). George Soros, a multi-billionaire investor, was among those who financed the successful 1998 ballot initiative campaigns. During the summer of 1998, the ONDCP's Drug Czar, General Barry R. McCaffrey, indirectly blamed Soros in a Senate testimonial. McCaffrey stated, "There is a carefully camouflaged, exorbitantly funded, well heeled elitist group whose ultimate goal is to legalize drug use in the United States" (Brooke, 1998).

Like Washington, Oregon's Measure 67 received approval in November 1998. As with the other state ballot initiatives, Measure 67 removed state level criminal penalties for users of medicinal marijuana. However, Measure 67 specified that medical marijuana patients, who did not previously register with the state as a marijuana patient, could claim an affirmative defense of medical necessity after arrest. As long as the accused person, hypothetically charged to be a criminal, did not possess more than three ounces of usable marijuana or three mature and four immature plants, the accused could legally use the affirmative defense of medical necessity. In doing so, the accused becomes a patient in the eyes of the court and avoids receiving the official label of criminal.

Alaska's Measure 8 also passed in November 1998 and resembled both of the Washington and Oregon measures (NORML, 2005). Like the Oregon law, the illnesses that the Alaska law earmarked for medicinal marijuana applications were Cachexia, cancer, chronic pain, epilepsy disorders, glaucoma, HIV/AIDS, MS, muscle spasticity, and nausea (MPP, 2004). Individuals, such as Mary Jane Defrank, an executive director of an ACLU chapter, rationalize such initiatives as Alaska's Measure 8 with statements such as, "In this instance, when you have people very, very ill, it is really the humane thing to allow them to use marijuana so they can keep their food down and keep their pills down" (Molotsky, 1999).

Commenting on the success of medical marijuana ballot initiatives, such as Alaska's, a spokesperson for the nonprofit Marijuana Policy Project, Chuck Thomas stated:

> To date, these initiatives have passed in every state in which they have appeared on the ballot...This confirms what every scientific public opinion poll has found since 1995: 60 to 80 percent of the American people support legal access to medicinal marijuana (Molotsky, 1999).

The above statement issued by MPP and reported upon by *The New York Times* is important in that it demonstrates that the medicinal marijuana social movement was increasingly employing the sovereign discourse of science to validate their claims that medical marijuana patients are normal and not criminal. This strategy has continued to work in favor of the non-profit organizations (NPOs) advocating for the medicalization of marijuana. In fact the Marijuana Policy Project, or MPP, viewed these ballot initiatives as Wave 1 of a Three Wave effort. Wave 2 involved lobbying state legislatures directly to vote on and pass state laws legalizing medicinal marijuana. Wave 3 involved a strategy referred to as de-federalization or removing marijuana from federal regulatory systems.

Standing in direct defiance of NPOs such as MPP or NORMAL was the old guard of tough on crime legislation. For one example among many, I use Republican Representative Bob Barr to illustrate those who represent the vestiges of marijuana prohibition. He states:

> The results . . . do not change my determination to insure that our nation's capital does not legalize any mind-altering drugs, including marijuana. Marijuana remains illegal under Federal law, and it would send a terrible message to America's young people to allow those laws to be openly flouted (Molotsky, 1999).

To de-emphasize Representative Barr's statement, Wayne Turner, leader of Act Up (an anti-AIDS group) states:

> Bob Barr has called it a hidden agenda and says that we want to legalize heroin and crack, but that's not so. The original sponsor was my partner, Steve Michael, who died of AIDS in 1998 . . . I am not a pot smoker and neither was he until a doctor told him to try marijuana to try to stimulate his appetite. He tried it and it worked. He stopped losing weight (Molotsky, 1999).

The Act-Up leader rebutted Representative Bob Barr's tough on crime statement with a smart on crime statement. In either statement, moral imperatives are clearly present. Both statements also reflect the way by which each claims maker views the immorality of the other. Lastly, both advocate a paternalistic or therapeutic approach to regulate the drug using proclivities of adult Americans.

Maine in 1999

The following year Maine's Question 2 passed in November 1999 (Goldberg, 2000). Maine required medicinal marijuana patients to possess an oral or written professional opinion from a licensed physician. As with similar state laws, penalties where removed for those patients using medicinal marijuana under their doctors' care. Legal protection was available to those with AIDS/HIV (for nausea/vomiting), cancer (for side effects associated with chemotherapy), MS, epilepsy, and glaucoma.

By 2000, prominent Mainers such as Sheriff Mark N. Dion of Cumberland County, Senator Anne M. Rand, as well as Representatives Lois A. Snowe-Mello and Thomas J. Kane were being quoted by the popular media (Goldberg, 2000). For example, Sheriff Dion went as far as to ask *The New York Times*, "Shall we as a sovereign state be held hostage by the federal government simply because we intend to treat our sick and afflicted?" The Maine Sheriff also stated that he should, "advocate for social justice when the law fails to meet the needs of its citizens" (Goldberg, 2000).

Hawaii, Nevada, and Colorado in 2000

Hawaii's medical marijuana legislation went into action in 2000. The law mimicked other state laws already in play, removing state level criminal penalties for those who qualified for medicinal marijuana prescriptions and for the usual conditions such as cancer, AIDS, and Crohn's disease. In addition, the law was typical in its restrictions of possession (one ounce for patients or their caregivers) and cultivation (three mature and four immature plants). The law also mandated that all patients be registered in a state run confidential registry and be in possession of identification cards (MPP, 2004).

However, the decriminalization of medical marijuana in Hawaii was an accomplishment of Hawaii's Legislature passing a bill, not by voters approving a medical marijuana ballot initiative. In the words of a MPP spokesperson, "We believe this is the second wave. Finally, we think the third wave will be the federal government" (Sterngold, 2000). Even the state's governor commented, "Hawaii joins a handful of forward thinking states that recognize the value and effectiveness of medical marijuana. We look forward to recognition on a federal level to provide relief to those suffering" (Sterngold, 2000).

In November 2000, the state of Nevada joined the growing ranks of states legalizing the medical use of marijuana when the voters of Nevada approved Question 9, thereby eliminating state level criminal penalties for medicinal marijuana users in Nevada, who possessed a doctor's prescription. Like the other measures, HIV/AIDS, cancer and glaucoma received earmarks for treatment. Like Nevada's Question 9, Colorado's Amendment 20 met with voter approval in November 2000 (MPP, 2004).

Vermont in 2004

Even though the Governor of Vermont, James Douglas, did not sign Senate Bill 76, the bill became law in May 2004, taking effect the following July. Like Hawaii's law, Vermont's law served to protect medicinal marijuana patients suffering from a debilitating medical condition. State level criminal penalties were rolled back for those diagnosed with AIDS, cancer, or MS and undergoing medicinal marijuana treatment. Like Hawaii, the Vermont law cast the second wave of medical marijuana legalization. As an aside, Montana voters approved their ballot initiative to legalize medical marijuana in November of 2004.

Analysis of State Laws: Medical Treatment as Social Control

Each deviant designation, either criminal or patient, carries with it its own separate, distinct and meaningful language. Although structurally similar in their origins, both deviant designations are the tips of two distinctly different icebergs. Each different label indicates the existence of a different complex of knowledge below the visible and "sayable" surface. Taken together, both deviant designations represent two different systems of citizen behavior regulation. Medicalization is nothing more than a process of deviant designation change; in the very same manner, that criminalization is nothing more than a process of deviant designation change.

Criminalization, as a practical method of social control for marijuana users is no longer as useful as it was during the mid-1900s. However, the potential for medicalization, as a practical method of social control, is becoming more acceptable as state governments continue to engage in ongoing efforts to find new and innovative ways to regulate the behavior of citizens through more pragmatic and fiscally conservative forms of subjectivities.

I employ a summary of nine state laws in Figure 5.1. This figure marshals two important pieces of evidence that policy makers often overlook. First, almost all of the states, with Vermont being the only exception, have approved medicinal marijuana as a treatment for the big three. By the big three, I mean Cancer, Glaucoma and AIDS/HIV. Very little socio-demographic data are available on those receiving and filling marijuana prescriptions. Nevertheless, all available data, that I was able to locate and review, indicate that pro-marijuana medicalization moral entrepreneurs use the big three medical conditions to leverage public opinion.

The big three argument calls attention to some of the unintended and undesirable consequences associated with extreme forms of marijuana prohibition. Policies that authorize state and federal agents to arrest, prosecute, and incarcerate terminally ill citizens, for self-medicating with marijuana, receive little support by the majority of voters. Nevertheless, while the big three may be the way claims makers sell a medical marijuana ballot initiative to mainstream American voters, the vast majority of medicinal marijuana prescriptions are not for these three conditions. Before discussing specifically what the vast majority of medicinal marijuana prescriptions are for, I must draw attention to the second important mechanism of these laws, rarely the subject of discussion.

Figure 5.1 – Medical Conditions Approved for Treatment with Marijuana in the First Nine States with Medical Marijuana Laws

	California	Oregon	Alaska	Washington	Maine	Hawaii	Colorado	Nevada	Vermont
Specific Diseases									
Cancer	●	●	●	●	●	●	●	●	●b
Glaucoma	●	●	●	●	●	●	●	●	
AIDS or HIV	●	●	●	●	●	●	●	●	●b
Crohn's Disease				●b,c					
Hepatitis C				●b,c					
Multiple Sclerosis									●b,c
Debilitating Medical Conditions or Symptoms Produced by the Conditions									
Cachexia, Anorexia or Wasting Syndrome	●	●	●	●b,c		●	●	●	
Severe or Chronic Pain	●	●	●	●b		●	●		
Severe or Chronic Nausea			●	●	●	●	●	●	
Seizure Disorders (e.g., epilepsy)			●	●	●	●	●	●	
Muscle Spasticity (e.g., multiple sclerosis)	●	●	●	●		●	●	●	

Figure 5.1 – Medical Conditions Approved for Treatment with Marijuana in the First Nine States with Medical Marijuana Laws (Continued)

	California	Oregon	Alaska	Washington	Maine	Hawaii	Colorado	Nevada	Vermont
Arthritis	●								
Migraines	●								
Agitation of Alzheimer's		●c							
Allows additions of Diseases or conditions by state health agency	●a	●	●	●		●	●	●	

a In addition to the specific diseases and conditions listed, the law covers treatment of "any other illness for which marijuana provides relief."
b Requires that medication available by prescription have failed to provide relief.
c Condition added by state agency

Source: MPP. 2004 *State-by-State Medical Marijuana Laws: How to Remove the Threat of Arrest.* Washington, D. C., Marijuana Policy Project.

With the exception of Maine and Vermont, medical marijuana laws specifically allow a state's respective health agency to add on diseases or conditions that might later, be determined to be treatable with marijuana. This open-ended clause is an important mechanism in achieving the larger goal of completely ending marijuana prohibition at the state level. For example, after an initiative passes and the high profile debate over medical marijuana calms down considerably, claims makers pursue the option to broaden medicinal marijuana treatments to include other ailments such as anxiety, stress or even depression. As a result, the deck shuffles again and the back door is left open for future low-profile policy dealings to take place. In this manner, recreational use of marijuana may be inserted into the status quo quietly and incrementally; much in the same way that marijuana prohibition was incrementally achieved.

Who Uses Medical Marijuana and Why?

The data indicate that the big three diseases are used to create or justify the need for the public to pass a medicinal marijuana ballot initiative. Additional diseases and medical problems may be added later to include less serious ailments. These findings raise additional questions: What are the demographic characteristics of the vast majority of those medical marijuana patients who are receiving prescriptions? In addition, what are the specific diseases or medical conditions most likely to be treated? While data on these medical marijuana patients are not readily available for all the states included in my analysis, some data associated with Nevada and Oregon are available to, in part, answer these questions.

The number of Oregonian medical marijuana patients, as seen in Figure 5.2, swelled from 594 patients in 2000 (the first year of program) to 3003 patients in 2002 (the third year of program). Thus, over these years, the medical marijuana patient population exploded fivefold. While the mean age remained stable (at 45 years old), as did the proportion of users who are male (70 percent), conditions such as severe pain, spasms and nausea made up for the vast majority of all prescriptions.

Between 2000 and 2002, the percentage of all users who received prescriptions for the big three diseases decreased threefold.

In sum, the data lead to the tentative conclusion that the typical or modal user of medicinal marijuana is an individual privileged enough to purchase intent and legitimacy while also avoiding the criminal label, as well as any hazardous black market risks. The description of the typical marijuana patient that is able to purchase medical intent while simultaneously dispensing with the arduous label of recreational drug user, is often a middle-aged male that claims to suffer from intense pain. The typical medicinal marijuana patient is not often a cancer or AIDS patient. Hence, I assert that the medical marijuana prescription primarily serves to protect status. As the law-abiding marijuana-using taxpayer experiences mid-life, the prescription insures societal privilege.

Thus, in the years after Oregonians passed the medical marijuana initiative, medical marijuana patients were coming out of the woodwork. These patients were, on average, middle-aged males with hard to verify complaints such as pain, spasms, and/or nausea. While the smaller proportion of big three patients were receiving the treatment they so desperately needed, most medical marijuana patients appear to be middle-aged males receiving what they wanted. Similar information is contained within Figure 5.3. Here, the number of medical marijuana patients in Nevada suffering from AIDS/HIV, cancer, or glaucoma is much smaller than the number of patients suffering from the hard to verify ailments of pain, spasms, and nausea.

**Figure 5.2 – Number of Patients Registered Under the Oregon
Medical Marijuana Program for Years 2000 and 2002**

Patient Characteristics	First Year (2000)	Third Year (2003)
Total Number	394	3,003
Average Age (range)	46 (14-87)	46 (18-87)
Male	415 (70%)	2,067 (68%)
Disease/Condition*		
Severe Pain	396 (67%)	1,760 (38%)
Spasms	243 (41%)	676 (23%)
Nausea	169 (29%)	154 (5%)
HIV	62 (10%)	98 (3%)
Cancer	54 (9%)	88 (3%)
Cachexia	44 (7%)	43 (1%)
Seizures	34 (6%)	71 (2%)
Glaucoma	16 (3%)	43 (1%)
Physicians participating	329	628
Counties with patients	31	34
Patients with caregiver	60%	60%

*Percentages may total more than 100% because many patients report multiple symptoms.
Source: MPP,. 2004. *State-By-State Medical Marijuana Laws: How to Remove the Threat of Arrest.*
Washington, D.C., Marijuana Policy Project, F-12.

**Figure 5.3 – Symptoms Reported by Patients in Nevada's
Medical Marijuana Registry Program (as of June 1, 2002)**

Disease or Condition	Number reported*
Severe Pain	109
Muscle Spasms	50
Severe Nausea	44
HIV/AIDS	27
Cachexia	24
Glaucoma	9
Cancer	8
Seizures	2

*Numbers total more than the 165 registered because many patients reported multiple symptoms.
Source: MPP,. 2004. *State-By-State Medical Marijuana Laws: How to Remove the Threat of Arrest.*
Washington, D.C., Marijuana Policy Project.

"Legalizing" Medical Marijuana: Three High Profile Court Cases

As a form of social control, marijuana medicalization already enjoys high levels of state sanctioned legitimacy and the activities of the states to medicalize marijuana is receiving attention by the nation's high courts. Three major high profile cases have made contemporary national headlines as the medicinal marijuana conflict seeks resolution through the courts. The volume of attention the medicinal marijuana debate has received from America's courts, since 1996, is considerable. However, the validity or invalidity of these petitions along with their associate rulings are inconsequential to the advancement of my inquiry. Nevertheless, the willingness or unwillingness of the nation's court systems to engage in the medicinal marijuana debate is of utmost importance to my contemporary inquiry.

United States v. Oakland Cannabis Buyers' Cooperative

After the voters of California passed Proposition 215 in 1996, a two-year legal battle began between the Oakland Cannabis Buyer's Cooperative (OCBC) and the United States. Eventually, the legal wrangling found its way to the nation's highest court. The federal government's tautological position was that, according to law, marijuana is a Schedule I drug. Therefore, according to its Schedule I classification, marijuana (by definition) has no medical use. The OCBC rebutted that the federal government had erroneously classified marijuana as a Schedule I drug. The OCBC argued that the federal government had used ambiguous reasoning when marijuana incorrectly received the classification of having no medicinal or therapeutic value. The federal government countered that, not only was there no medicinal benefits to be derived by ill citizens using marijuana to relieve their suffering, patients could use existing and legal medications that made use of synthetic versions of the active ingredients found with *cannabis-sativa*. To rebut, OCBC contended that the federal government was ignoring the therapeutic potential of marijuana and was preventing patients who were seriously ill, and suffering, from receiving and using medicinal marijuana.

The case against the Oakland Cannabis Buyers' Cooperative was the result of the federal government's aggressive campaign to shut down thirteen California based distributors of medicinal marijuana. These thirteen distributors began to operate openly and in defiance of federal law after the passage of Proposition 215. After these marijuana distribution centers began to operate independently, the United States filed a separate lawsuit against each of the medicinal marijuana supply clubs. Ultimately, in 1998, a U.S. District Court heard the government's case against the Cannabis Cultivator's Club in *United States* v. *Cannabis Cultivators Club,* 5 F. Supp. 2d 1086, 1092 (ND Cal. 1998). The court ruled that the medical necessity or medically necessary defense was not an acceptable defense. Because of the 1998 ruling, ten of the clubs closed their doors, stopping operations. However, the OCBC was defiant of the court's rulings.

The Oakland Cannabis Buyer's Cooperative continued to openly engage in civil disobedience and distribute medicinal marijuana despite the legal order they received from the federal government to close down their operation. The OCBC tried an unusual legal route to defend their operation. The Oakland-based cooperative filed two motions and did not file an appeal. While one motion claimed that the OCBC was immune from liability under federal law, the other motion asked for permission from the federal government to distribute medicinal marijuana to patients with a doctor's certificate.

Judge Charles Breyer denied the request by OCBC to continue operating, ruling that OCBC failed to prove that the federal government's actions were violating the rights of the sick to relieve their ailments with marijuana. Judge Breyer asserted that the OCBC and its membership violated an earlier federal injunction against the cannabis collective by continuing to distribute marijuana. Two hours before federal marshals padlocked the doors of the OCBC, OCBC employees voluntarily closed their doors and gave away trays of marijuana plants to the patients they were serving. Despite the loss, OCBC appealed Judge Breyer's decision.

In 1999, The Ninth Circuit Court of Appeals reversed Judge Breyer's decision. The medicinal marijuana social movement found new hope when the Ninth Circuit ordered Judge Breyer to review his 1998 decision against the OCBC. The Ninth Circuit's 3-0 decision indicated that the medical necessity defense protected patients that could prove that marijuana was an indispensable component of their overall health care needs. The Ninth Circuit forced Breyer to amend his ruling so that cannabis clubs could begin distributing marijuana again for those who were in medical need. Consequently, the federal government's appeal of the Ninth Circuit's ruling was heard by the nation's highest court.

In 2001 the Supreme Court unanimously overturned the Ninth Circuit , and upheld the District Court's ruling against OCBC in *United States v. Oakland Cannabis Buyers' Cooperative* , 532 US 483 (2001).

Conant v. Walters

The second major legal battle associated with today's medicinal marijuana social movement centered on the California physician, Dr. Marcus Conant, and the Director of National Drug Control Policy or America's Drug Czar, John P. Walters. Like *Oakland Cannabis Buyers' Cooperative, Conant v. Waters* began in California after the passage of Proposition 215. However, the legal battle between Dr. Conant and America's Drug Czar continued into 2003. Conant argued that the federal government was violating his First Amendment right to free speech. More specifically, the California physician argued that the First Amendment protected him from federal efforts to prevent physicians from discussing and recommending marijuana as a treatment option to patients. The nation's Drug Czar, John P. Walters, argued that Conant's actions amounted to a Schedule I drug violation. Walters argued that any physician who recommended marijuana to his or her patients threatened the safety and health of the American people. As a rebuttal, Conant argued that, as a physician, he needed to have the ability to interact fully and honestly with his patients as he recommended all available treatment options that may be useful.

Conant, an AIDS/HIV specialist working out of San Francisco, brought his suit against the federal government, with assistance from the ACLU, medicinal marijuana advocacy groups, activist doctors, and even medicinal marijuana patients. Conant argued that the Bush Administration and the DEA were acting outside of their sphere of authority when they threatened to withdraw the prescription licenses of California doctors who recommended marijuana as a treatment option to their patients. In addition, the federal government threatened to take away physicians' Medicaid and Medicare status should they be caught recommending medicinal marijuana. During this period, the Bush Administration also threatened physicians with federal indictments and criminal prosecution for aiding and abetting the prescription of marijuana.

Under the Anti-Drug Legislation of 1986 and the Conspiracy Amendment of 1988, these activist doctors could potentially receive harsh federal mandatory sentences regardless of their history (or total lack thereof) of criminal activity. In other words, physicians who were caught by federal law enforcement agents recommending or writing prescriptions for medicinal marijuana in states such as California, could be in violation of harsh federal drug conspiracy laws. During this period of time, and under certain circumstances, these doctors could have been indicted, tried and sentenced by federal prosecutors and potentially could have received life sentences without hope of parole.

Even if the activist physicians were first time non-violent offenders, under federal conspiracy charges, they could receive harsh punishments. These draconian federal laws, passed at the height of the drug war in 1986, were empowered in 1988 when Congress passed another pre-November Anti-Drug Law. The 1988 Anti-Drug Legislation and the 1988 Conspiracy Amendment empowered federal prosecutors to make everyone involved in the said conspiracy liable for every act said to be committed during the entire conspiracy. In other words, if a doctor introduced a patient to a medicinal marijuana distribution club, that physician could be liable for all of the marijuana that the patient and the marijuana cooperative had ever bought or sold. In this scenario, the doctor could be liable for all of the marijuana the medicinal marijuana distribution cooperative had ever or would ever manufacture, distribute or sell. Conant was reacting to very real threats by the Bush Administration to hold activist California physicians responsible for all the marijuana ever sold from the Oakland-based collective.

Dr. Conant felt that the government had overstepped its legal and moral authority and had acquired too much authority. Since then, the Supreme Court ruled that certain federal mandatory minimum sentencing laws were unconstitutional and could only recommend sentencing guidelines to federal judges. Nevertheless, during the *Conant v. Walters* dispute, the Bush Administration's threat to arrest and prosecute doctors with harsh sentences was not an idle threat to be easily dismissed.

Conant argued that if physicians did not act to protect their administrative and professional turf, the federal government would continue to take power away from physicians. He believed that over time physicians would not be able to practice medicine as they deemed appropriate. Conant also argued that it was the professional as well as moral duty of physicians to stand up to a federal government that was behaving irresponsibly and recklessly with power. Conant posited that the federal government had behaved in a similar manner in the past as federal officials struggled to gain administrative turf over politically volatile medical topics such as abortion and birth control.

Conant argued that the courts had been used successfully in the past to limit the authority of the government to censor what doctors could tell patients about abortion. Additionally, Conant argued that in the past the courts helped change the actions of government officials who had sought to stop physicians from writing prescriptions to women for birth control pills or what many at the time referred to as The Pill. In the words of Dr. Conant: "Physicians at times need to stand up and say that the government is wrong" (Albert, 2002).

While resolute, Conant was not alone in his legal battle. The CEO of the California Medical Association, Dr. Jack Lewin, filed an amicus brief and alleged that the Bush Administration and the DEA were jeopardizing patient care while also censoring the free speech of California physicians. Dr. Lewin argued, "The federal government is acting emotionally rather than logically, intruding on the physician-patient relationship" (Albert, 2002).

The heavy-handed approach to dealing with physicians who prescribed medicinal marijuana was not unique to the Bush Administration. For example in 1996, the Clinton Administration emphasized the policy that any physicians who prescribed marijuana were in danger of having their prescription registrations revoked. After the Clinton Administration made their stance against medicinal marijuana widely known, the editor of the New England Journal of Medicine, Jerome P. Kassirer stated, "federal officials are out of step with the public" (Lee, 2004). Additionally, Dr. Kassirer referred to the Clinton Administration's crackdown against doctors who recommend medical marijuana as "misguided, heavy-handed and inhumane" (Lee, 2004). Originally, the Conant case emerged to challenge Clinton's federal crackdown as physicians and patients began to coalesce into special interest groups and grass roots non-profit entities. These groups found support from the ACLU as they began to sue the federal government. I emphasize these details because the federal government's contemporary stance against medical marijuana under Bush's Republican Presidential Administration originally emerged under Clinton's Democratic Presidential Administration. In sum, the federal government's hard line against medicinal marijuana had enjoyed bipartisan support.

In July 2000, a U.S. District Judge handed Conant and the medicinal marijuana movement a victory in the form of a permanent injunction against the federal government in *Conant v. McCaffrey*, 2000 WL 1281174 (N.D. Cal. Sept. 7, 2000).

The injunction forced federal law enforcement to respect the right of physicians to discuss treatment options such as medicinal marijuana with their patients. The federal government appealed the decision to the Ninth Circuit Court of Appeals only to lose again in October of 2002 in *Conant v. Walters*, 309 F.3d 629

(9th Cir. 2002). Once again, the federal government appealed the decision and sought a hearing with the nation's highest court.

In October 2003, a year after the Ninth Circuit ruled in favor of physicians' rights, the Supreme Court refused to hear the government's appeal. As a result, the medicinal marijuana movement in America was quietly handed its first major victory. Solicitor General Theodore Olson, John Walter's attorney, argued, "The decision impairs the Executive's authority to enforce the law in an area vital to the public health and safety" (Jones, 2003). In addition, Olson stated, "The practice of medicine is subject to reasonable licensing and regulation, even where that practice involves speech" (Jones, 2003). However, at the end of the day, Dr. Conant's free speech argument prevailed as the courts responded favorably to the physicians' arguments to protect their administrative turf from federal law enforcement agencies. Conant summarized one of the primary epistemological concerns associated with his legal battle when he declared, "Let's draw the line here...Science should decide medicine, not the government" (Albert, 2002). According to Conant, the sovereign discourse of science should govern the medical industrial complex, not federal law enforcement claims makers.

Raich v. Ashcroft

Once again, in 2002, the State of California played host to a major legal dispute associated with the nation's medicinal marijuana debate. The *Raich v. Ashcroft* case surfaced in 2002 when a group of Californians was charged by federal law enforcement for violating anti-drug legislation. In August 2002, the DEA raided the residence of Diana Monson where Angel Raich was living. Angel Raich was the wife of an OCBC lawyer, Robert Raich. Robert Raich and company were responsible for handing federal law enforcement their first major public relations defeat over medical marijuana in the OCBC legal dispute.

By October 2002, all six were involved in a suit against Attorney General John Ashcroft and the DEA. Raich charged that the federal government violated their fifth, ninth and tenth Amendment rights. In addition, their suit charged that their rights had been violated under the Commerce Clause of Article 1 of the Constitution. Raich argued that the nation's General Attorney had overstepped his legal authority by engaging in a campaign to seize intrastate medical marijuana, privately grown by patients and caregivers inside the state of California. Raich contended that Ashcroft and company had violated civil and administrative law by harassing, raiding, arresting and prosecuting Raich and company.

Angel Raich's diagnoses included an inoperable brain tumor and wasting disease. Raich was using marijuana regularly to relieve the symptoms of these illnesses. Raich's story was a modern-day horror story about the evils associated with contemporary marijuana prohibition and was nothing less than an important turning point in the new war against marijuana prohibition. The federal government was cast as callus and cruel as it sought to prosecute medicinal marijuana users.

After losing in District Court in *Raich v. Ashcroft*, 248 F. Supp. 2d 918 (ND Cal. 2003), Raich filed an appeal in March 2003 with the Ninth Circuit Court of Appeals and Raich's prosecution was publicly recast as Raich's persecution. The Ninth Circuit Court reversed the decision by the district court in *Raich v. Ashcroft*, 352 F. 3d 1222 (2003), and rejected the Department of Justice's petition for an *en banc* review of the decision. However, in 2004, the Supreme Court agreed to hear the case. By November 2004, the Supreme Court heard the oral arguments associated with *Raich v. Ashcroft*. In 2005, the Supreme Court ruled against Raich.

Summary Discussion of the Three High Profile Court Cases

It is important to emphasize that today's federalized form of marijuana prohibition did not result from the passage of an amendment to the U.S. Constitution, like the prohibition of alcohol. Now, the constitutional authority of federal law enforcement to prohibit marijuana is currently under question within this arena of contested public policy. Relying upon legal justifications associated with interstate commerce, the federal government has left itself vulnerable to legal arguments defending the legitimate use of medicinal marijuana within state borders where marijuana collectives distribute the drug without buying or selling. As a result, those using medicinal marijuana, growing plants on their own land, and not selling the drug, might have already created an end-run around the federal government's legal authority to prohibit marijuana. If marijuana had been prohibited by the passage of a Constitutional amendment (as was done during alcohol prohibition); the federal government would, without question, retain its authority to prohibit medicinal and recreational uses of marijuana in the face of any state level legislative contradiction. However, since the prohibitive tax route was pursued in 1937, the federal prohibition on marijuana seems to be built upon a less than stable legal foundation. As a result, contemporary medicinal marijuana activist groups, such as MPP and NORML, may continue to exploit the constitutionally questionable character inherent in federal policing efforts to prohibit marijuana.

The Nine Descriptions from the Genealogy

In an effort to make the genealogical method more accessible, I break the entire process of inquiry down into nine distinct questions. According to Kendall and Wickham (2000: 34), these nine questions are as follows:

- What is the web of discourse?
- How can the statements be described while emphasizing power?
- What is the problem of the present?
- How do the statements facilitate an on-going practice?
- How can power be described through the history of the present?
- How can contemporary analyses be made uncomfortable?
- What are the disreputable origins of the processual movement?
- What are the unpalatable functions of the processual movement?
- How are these statements analogous to moving pictures?

By answering these questions, I demonstrate that medicalization, as a discourse, is productive. By productive, I mean that the discourse of marijuana medicalization produces medical marijuana patients. For example, the medicinal marijuana patient did not really exist before California passed Proposition 215 in 1996. Importantly, I am not claiming that, pre-1996, there were no Americans using marijuana to self-medicate for a variety of reasons. I am claiming that the contemporary discourse of marijuana medicalization has produced and reproduced the official concept and the legitimized label of the medical marijuana patient literally thousands of times after 1996.

Using marijuana to medicate other individuals or to self-medicate is not a new development in American history. However, the way by which the discourse of marijuana medicalization began, after 1996, to appropriate large numbers of individuals and their behaviors is astonishing. So, what are the basic tenets associated with the discourse of the medicinal marijuana (post 1996) in America? Who are the key players in the medicinal marijuana movement? Who are the prime targets for receiving these legitimizing labels? How are these labels justified in the first place? How is the application of these labels standardized over time? To answer questions such as these, I continue the analysis.

Describing the Web of Discourse

To view pro/con medicinal marijuana statements as the products of simple coercive discursive systems is reasonable at the present juncture. Products of old or out-of-date models of discursive machinery (i.e., old or clichéd statements) may be viewed by contemporary consumers of information as out of touch or ignorant. Products of the newest model of discursive machinery, or medicalization, may then be encouraged to champion the agendas and language of the supporters of medicalization. Thereby, claims makers may assert their own personal and/or group values and interests as the best model for all citizens to adopt and follow. Should marijuana medicalization increasingly move into vogue, the preceding discourse of marijuana criminalization might increasingly be characterized as non-useable, or even inept, immoral, irresponsible and unable to produce systematic justice.

Medicalization, like criminalization, employs its own distinct set of definitions and statements. Each new set of definitions and labels (belonging to the newest coercive discursive formation) positions itself to destroy the past closed discursive system (i.e., criminalization) through paradigmatic warfare. The definitions associated with the successful implementation of the previous discursive entity and its passé mechanisms of subjectivity are tailor made for individuals from a past temporal location. The newest system of symbolic or grammatical fashion (i.e., medicalization) can be, over time, brought into today's history, marketed as culturally and intellectually preferred. This would push a newly legitimated superstructure of truth to move into vogue through widespread agreement and enthusiastic anticipation.

Describing Statements while Emphasizing Power

Through the invariable production of visibilities (i.e., via marijuana prohibition horror stories), the newest brand of truth becomes normalized and uncontroversial. Hyperactive production of pro-medicalization visibilities may then undergo replication along with the pro-medicalization statements, which initially produced the visibilities. As these visibilities and statements enter into high levels of reproduction and public consumption, the visibilities and statements experience gradual privilege, and transform into agreed upon truisms.

The exponential production of visibilities is, in and of itself, a by-product of the discursive machinery that had initially borne out its invented necessities. Here, a self-fulfilling prophecy of sorts takes place. For example, social actors must first receive coaching on how to see the symptoms of marijuana prohibition before they can become advocates for the cure, medicalizing marijuana. The use of horror stories instructs a naïve public on how to identify and verify marijuana prohibition as the cause of many contemporary social problems. This is how the claims makers of the medicinal marijuana movement recast the entire pro/con marijuana debate to their distinct advantage. By illustrating marijuana prohibition as the cause of the disease, and by specifying the disease as institutionalized immorality, horror stories of overzealous anti-drug law enforcement activities easily transform into symptoms for the lay population to diagnose. As a result, a newly educated public effortlessly identifies suitable statements and visibilities as symptoms.

Describing the Problem of the Present

Medicalization exists within the information marketplace as the cure for the disease of marijuana prohibition, whereby, new public policy recommendations eliminate the symptoms of marijuana prohibition. For example, if a doctor gives a prescription to a patient so that s/he may legally use marijuana then the doctor is preventing the individual from ever having to interact with the criminal justice system. Public opinion seems to favor giving physicians the authority to prescribe medicinal marijuana with some restrictions. The impact on changing public opinion (i.e., the normalization of the marijuana using societal actor) has a direct impact on how the individual interacts within his/her social order. The impact of changing the social atmosphere that envelops the marijuana-using individual has largely gone unnoticed within the debate over medical marijuana. If the laws change then the social settings change and once the social settings change, individuals usually feel the impulse to move with change. Some national and state level opinion polls are summaries below in Figures 5.4 and 5.5.

As Figures 5.4 and 5.5 demonstrate, high levels of support exist for decriminalizing medicinal marijuana at the state and national level. The data indicate that the paradigmatic shift toward medicalizing marijuana is already over. Public policy officials and academics specializing in drug policy may very well be the last to catch up with public opinion, as NPOs such as MPP enter into the driver's seat.

Describing Statements as an On-Going Practice

Within the divide of public sensibilities and public policies, the medical marijuana campaign legitimizes its own claims as the public is encouraged to reflect upon the greater evil of incarcerating nonviolent offenders, at the taxpayers' expense. In the words of MPP's Executive Director, Rob Kampia (2004):

> Why should recreational smokers get behind medical marijuana? For the same reasons non-pot smokers get behind medical marijuana. Some 75 percent of the population doesn't believe patients should be put in jail, and I would hope that recreational users would actually work on this issue. But I don't really view the medical marijuana

> issue through the lens of the recreational smoker, I look at it through the lens of how many people can we keep out of prison in the short run and let's not hurt our chances in the long run. Medical marijuana is a worthwhile issue on its face, the lobbying is relatively inexpensive; there is no downside.

Kampia's statement reflects a larger shift in public knowledge about marijuana. The resulting discursive shift from criminalizing marijuana to medicalizing marijuana may be more than symbolic in its reallocation; from a traditional form of government sanctioned patriarchal hard power to a new emphasis on government sanctioned matriarchal soft power.

Medicalization of now prohibited recreational substances may very well be the next lesser evil cost saving public policy initiative to supplant the correctional industrial complex's attempts to manage the 500,000 plus non-violent offenders serving time for violations of federal and state anti-drug legislation. As officials of public policy work to reformulate drug policy in America, the broken promises of modernity receive a new coat of paint. Here, the promises of modernity are on sale yet again, for the American public to buy. The same strategy was in play during the early years of marijuana criminalization. Medicalization, like criminalization, provides a prefabricated and familiar structure or framework of ready-made public policy solutions associated with citizen behavior regulation.

Figure 5.4 – The Medical Marijuana Public Opinion Polling Results:
First Nine States which Legalized the Use of Medical Marijuana

State	Date	% in Favor	Margin of error	No. of respondents	Wording	Polling firm/ where reported
Alaska	Feb. 2003	74	+ or - 2.6% to 3.1%	Between 1,004 and 1,464 adults	"What is your level of support for the current medical marijuana law?"	Lucas Organization and Arlington Research Group, on behalf of MPP
California	Jan. 2004	74	+ or - 4.5%	500 registered voters	"Do you favor or oppose implementation of Proposition 215, to allow for the medical use of marijuana in California?"	Field Research poll
Colorado	Feb. 2002	77	+ or - 2.6% to 3.1%	Between 1,004 and 1,464 adults	"What is your level of support for the current medical marijuana law?"	
Hawaii	Feb. 3-12, 2000	77	+ or - 3.7%	703 registered voters	Favor "the Hawaii State Legislature passing a law in Hawaii to allow seriously or terminally ill patients to use marijuana for medical purposes if supported by their medical doctor"	QMark Research & Polling on behalf of the Drug Policy Forum of Hawaii

Figure 5.4 – The Medical Marijuana Public Opinion Polling Results: First Nine States which Legalized the Use of Medical Marijuana (Continued)

State	Date	% in Favor	Margin of error	No. of respondents	Wording	Polling firm/ where reported
Maine	Oct. 1999	68	+ or - 4%	400	Support legalizing marijuana for medical use under a doctor's supervision	Bangor Daily News/ WCSH 6 Poll, reported in The People Have Spoken
Nevada	Feb. 2002	79	+ or - 2.6% to 3.1%	Between 1,004 and 1,464 adults	"What is your level of support for the current medical marijuana law?"	Lucas Organization and Arlington Research Group on behalf of MPP
Oregon: Data unavailable						
Vermont	Mar. 19-22, 2004	71	+ or - 4.5%	502 randomly selected voters	Support pending legislation "to allow people with cancer, AIDS, and other serious illnesses to use and grow their own marijuana for medical purposes, so long as their physician approves."	Zogby International on behalf of the MPP
Washington: Data unavailable						

Source: MPP. 2004 *State-by-State Medical Marijuana Laws: How to Remove the Threat of Arrest.* Washington, D. C., Marijuana Policy Project.

Figure 5.5 – Nationwide Medical Marijuana Public Opinion Polling Results

Date	% in Favor	Margin of error	No. of respondents	Wording	Polling firm/where reported
Nov. 2002	80	+ or - 3.1%	1,007 adults	"Do you think adults should be allowed to legally use marijuana for medical purposes if their doctors prescribe it?"	Harris Interactive for Time Magazine
Jan. 2002	70	N/A	N/A	"Should medical marijuana be allowed?"	Center for Substance Abuse Research, Univ of Maryland
Mar. 2001	73	+ or - 3%	1,513 adults	"Regardless of what you think about the person non medical use of marijuana, do you think doctors should or should not be allowed to prescribe marijuana for medical purposes to treat their patients?"	Pew Research Center
Mar. 19-21, 1999	73	+ or - 5%	1,018 adults	Support "making marijuana legally available for doctors to prescribe in order to reduce pain and suffering"	Gallup
Sep. 7-21, 1997	62	N/A	N/A	Favor legalizing marijuana "strictly for medical use"	The Little Research Companies for Merrill Lynch and Wired Magazine
May 27, 1997	69	+ or - 4.5%	517 adults	Support "legalizing medical use of marijuana"	Chilton Research, on behalf of ABC News/Discovery News

Figure 5.5 – Nationwide Medical Marijuana Public Opinion Polling Results (Continued)

Date	% in Favor	Margin of error	No. of respondents	Wording	Polling firm/where reported
Feb. 5-9, 1997	60	N/A	1,002 registered voters	"Do you favor allowing doctors to prescribe marijuana for medical purposes for seriously ill or terminal patients?"	Lake Research on behalf of the Lindesmith Center
Feb. 5-9, 1997	68	N/A	1,002 registered voters	"The federal government should not penalize physicians who prescribe marijuana regardless of whether state laws permit it."	Lake Research on behalf of the Lindesmith Center
1997	66-Independent 64-Democrats 57-Republicans	N/A	Responses divided among party affiliations	"Doctors should be allowed to prescribe small amounts of marijuana for patients suffering serious illnesses."	CBS News/The New York Times
1997	74	+ or - 2.8%	1,000 registered voters	"People who find that marijuana is effective for their medical condition should be able to use it legally."	Commissioned by the Family Research Council
1995	79	+ or - 3.1%	1,001 registered voters	"It would be a good idea . . . to legalize marijuana to relieve pain and for other medical uses if prescribed by a doctor."	Belden & Russonelle on behalf of the American Civil Liberties Union

Source: MPP 2004. *State-By-State Marijuana Laws: How to Remove the Threat of Arrest.* Washington, D. C.: Marijuana Policy Report.

Medicalization de-emphasizes physical incapacity and material surveillance and the acceptance of internalized chemical surveillance moves into vogue. The government consequently produces an acceptable compromise, holding on to its parental base of authority through the employment of maternal and therapeutic authority and power. As a result, the government offers up medical science as the sovereign discursive mechanism by which the ills of society are to be cured. Medicalization purports to accomplish what criminalization failed to accomplish; namely, the efficient and economic production of a responsible, yet free citizenry.

Describing Power through the History of the Present

Parallels might be drawn from past efforts associated with early state level marijuana criminalization (i.e., 1911-1917) with contemporary efforts associated with state level marijuana medicalization (i.e., 1996-2004). Numerous states criminalized marijuana before the federal government made marijuana virtually illegal in 1937. Some of the initial states and the years in which they criminalized marijuana are as follows: Massachusetts, 1911; California, 1913; Maine, 1913; Wyoming, 1913; Indiana, 1913; Utah, 1915; Vermont, 1915, Colorado, 1917; Nevada 1917 (Gieringer, 1999). Likewise, some of the earliest states to pass medicinal marijuana initiatives are as follows: California, 1996; Oregon, 1998; Washington (State), 1998; Maine, 1999; Alaska, 1999; Colorado, 2000; Hawaii, 2000; Nevada, 2000; and Vermont, 2004.

During the early 1910s, the early state laws that criminalized marijuana (1911-1917) did not cause the federal government to pass the Marijuana Tax Act of 1937. Likewise, the first nine contemporary state laws that medicalized marijuana (1996-2004) will not cause federal lawmakers to pass a marijuana medicalization act in the near future. In sum, the contemporary trend among the states to legalize the medicinal use of marijuana serves only to locate one of many different contingencies associated with likelihood of a potential shift in federal law.

**Figure 5.6 – Parallels of State Process as Precursors
to Federal Legislative Action**

State Criminalization Laws (1915-1927)		State Medicalization Laws (1996-2004)	
State	**Year**	**State**	**Year**
Massachusetts	1911	California	1996
California	1913	Oregon	1998
Wyoming	1913	Washington	1998
Maine	1913	Maine	1999
Indiana	1913	Alaska	1999
Utah	1915	Colorado	2000
Vermont	1915	Hawaii	2000
Colorado	1917	Nevada	2000
Nevada	1917	Vermont	2004
Federal Level Medical Marijuana "Criminalization" Through the passage of The Marijuana Tax Act of 1937		Federal Level Marijuana "Medicalization" through the passage of _____.	

Making Uncomfortable Existing Analyses

Today's medicinal marijuana claims makers may not be very different from those who lobbied to criminalize marijuana more than seven decades ago. If Anslinger was the premier claims maker for marijuana criminalization, Rob Kampia might be today's premier claims maker for the contemporary medicalization of marijuana movement. Kampia's organization, The Marijuana Policy Project (MPP), a large non-profit organization out of Washington D.C., regularly batches out personal email updates from Kampia to all of MPP's membership. By lobbying legislative bodies, MPP dramatically affects state and federal drug legislation. Bills, which might restrict the federal government's initiatives to prosecute medicinal marijuana users, receive support. Bills, which conflict with MPP's marijuana medicalization agenda, are actively discouraged. An example of one of Kampia's many emails is as follows:

Late yesterday, July 7 [2004], the U.S. House of Representatives defeated by a vote of 148-268 an amendment that would have prevented the DEA and the U.S. Justice Department from spending any more money to raid and prosecute medical marijuana patients and providers. This is only the second time in history that the full House has voted on binding legislation to end the federal government's war on medical marijuana. (The U.S. Senate never has.) Although we lost, yesterday's vote was an impressive showing, in large part because of the letters that members and allies of the Marijuana Policy Project have been faxing to their United States Representatives. MPP generated thousands of messages to Capitol Hill – including more than 5,000 in just the past week – showing United States House members the collective strength of the medical marijuana grassroots movement (Kampia, 2004).

Those who have signed up for email updates receive bulk emails from Kampia and MPP, almost daily. However, MPP is not the only nonprofit organization interested in medicalizing marijuana. Additional organizations are also assertively using Internet resources to mobilize and empower their respective anti drug-war non-profit networks (i.e., Richard Lake's DPFCO; DRCNet; NORML; and FAMM). Rob Kampia's information machine is only one of the many NPOs working aggressively and at times very creatively and effectively, to change state and federal laws that prohibit citizens from legally using medicinal marijuana.

Describing and Analyzing Disreputable Origins

The role that the Internet plays within contemporary public policy debate cannot be over-emphasized. For example, after a reader of one of MPP's emails takes in Kampia's most recent pep talk, the email recipient is encouraged to donate money. The emails urge recipients to send off a prewritten letter to their appropriate representative. If their home state representative did not vote in favor of medicinal marijuana legislation, the email recipient is encouraged to hit a link that sends out a SPANK letter. If the email recipient's representative did vote in favor of medicinal marijuana legislation, the email recipient is encouraged to hit a link that sends out a THANK letter.

The impact felt by state representatives is immense. Over time, these NPO memberships discipline state and federal lawmakers like a parent disciplines a child. Eventually, the child craves praise from the parent and fears punishment. After a period, the child internalizes the will of her/his watchful parent. Likewise, the Marijuana Policy Project encourages its list membership (by mid 2004, MPP boasted 150,000 members) as well as dues paying membership (over 50,000) to engage directly with their representative's office through massive, organized and synchronized Internet emailing and faxing. For example, some of the content contained in a typical SPANK letter is as follows:

> Your decision to allow the federal government to continue arresting the seriously ill leaves me deeply saddened. On July 7, you cast a vote against the Farr-Rohrabacher amendment during consideration of the Commerce-Justice-State Appropriations bill. Your vote in favor of increasing the suffering of patients suffering AIDS, cancer, and MS is simply deplorable. Your vote is also out of step with the 80 percent of Americans that polls like the Time/CNN (Oct 2002) poll show support access to medical marijuana. Your vote shows your disregard of the voters and legislators in the nine states that have chosen to protect medical marijuana patients and comprise 20 percent of the population in the United States. Your vote is dismissive to organizations that have endorsed medical marijuana like the 2.6 million-member American Nurses Association, the eight million-member United Methodist Church, and the editorial board of The New England Journal of Medicine. I am ashamed of your vote to continue the arrest and prosecutions of the sick and dying (MPP, 2004).

The language of a SPANK letter carries with it, righteous indignation, aimed at any political representative who voted against whatever legislative initiative the non-profit organization advocated.

If the email recipient from the MPP list-serve lives in an area of the country, whereby their political representative voted for a legislative initiative that the pro-marijuana NPO favored, a letter is then generated to THANK the appropriate political representative. Below is one example of the many different pre-written letters that are available to the politically conscious email recipient who might send out a THANK letter to his or her political representative:

> Your vote demonstrates your awareness of the importance of ending these needless arrests of patients suffering with AIDS, cancer, and MS. Your vote is also in line with the 80 percent of Americans who support patients having access to medical marijuana. If you have not done so already, please consider cosponsoring H.R. 2233, which would recognize states' rights to regulate the use of medical marijuana, and H.R. 1717, which would allow an affirmative defense for the use of medical marijuana. I look forward to your continued support and defense of the seriously ill (MPP, 2004).

All it takes is an extra minute or two and the recipient can point and click a THANK or SPANK letter to their representative.

These computer-generated letters are prefabricated statements produced and reproduced on a massive scale by many different NPOs, not just MPP. Tens of thousands of these Internet letters are not the statements of tens of thousands of different constituents voicing their pro-medical marijuana views to their representatives. These letters are the voice of a very small number of moral entrepreneurs; however, virtual spam communiqué amplify these few voices by the tens of thousands.

Describing and Analyzing Unpalatable Functions

The medical marijuana issue may be a hot button topic because it is being leveraged to serve as a lynch pin issue to end America's drug war. These THANK and SPANK letters are influential because they take place simultaneously and on a massive scale, regardless of the issue addressed. Obviously, different non-profit organizations have different numbers of members. Nevertheless, when a large number of NPOs gravitate to one particular issue, such as medicalizing marijuana, their creative and relentless campaigning can sway legislative bodies. The synergistic impact of multiple non-profits acting simultaneously and temporarily, as one cohesive and assertive voice to support or hinder the passage of legislation, is considerable.

Bulk emails, such as Kampia's, ask for donations for their congressional lobbying efforts. While sometimes under-funded, these non-profit legalization entities can spend large sums on thousands of hours lobbying for legislative support. To illustrate, an excerpt of a bulk email is as follows:

> On June 4, we organized more than 500 MPP members, medical marijuana patients, caregivers, and other supporters in protests at 110 congressional district offices, urging targeted members of Congress to support the amendment. The protests generated news coverage nationwide and forced many legislators to come face-to-face with medical marijuana patients who are suffering under the policies the legislators have voted for. And last week, MPP brought TV host Montel Williams – who uses medical marijuana to treat symptoms of multiple sclerosis – to Capital Hill to address a packed room of almost 200 congressional staffers about the proposal (Kampia, 2004).

The above bulk email from the non-profit MPP goes on to explain how legislators, who do not vote in line with the MPP agenda, are targeted for and disciplined by a "massive public awareness campaign among their constituents – with the hope that those legislators will pay the price at the polls on November 2. And now we're going to make good on that promise" (Kampia, 2004). Kampia goes on to explain in the email that a smear campaign is to begin, and continue through summer and into the upcoming fall.

Districts that are home to the unfortunate legislator that voted against MPP's recommendation (and quite possibly voted according to how the majority of his or her constituency would have preferred him or her to vote) are to be the target of a poster campaign. Kampia states,

> with posters designed to look like the front page of a tabloid, with the headline 'Congressman *(name inserted here)* votes to send cancer patients to jail; these posters cost only two cents to produce . . . and we've budgeted enough to distribute 250,000 of the fliers in every targeted district (Kampia, 2004).

While "postering" is only one of the many different tactics used by the NPOs, Kampia and other contemporary medical marijuana claims makers have persistently and successfully reframed their own agenda as a moral imperative for all Americans to passionately adopt, as did William Bennett (during the 1980's) or Harry Anslinger (during the 1930s). However, Kampia and the other claims making reformers derive the vast majority of their funding from private donations; Bennett and Anslinger's coffers were full of federal taxpayers' dollars.

Kampia's foresight to use disciplinary power to affect the behavior of representatives may be superior to past complaint-only styles of special interest campaigning. In so doing, MPP not only punishes the undisciplined politician who disobeys; MPP rewards the representative who votes in line with MPP's agenda. Over time, representatives that deviate from the agendas of the pro-marijuana NPOs learn to fear voting against their recommendation. In addition, politicians desire praise from the anti-prohibition NPOs. Eventually, state and federal lawmakers seek to please the drug policy reformers. Whether or not these legislators consciously or unconsciously seek out the reformers' praise is inconsequential.

Describing Statements as Motion Pictures

MPP utilizes celebrity personalities such as comedian Jack Black, ex-professional wrestler and former governor Jesse Ventura, and former U.S. Surgeon General Jocelyn Elders who vocally support campaigns to medicalize marijuana. The medicalization of marijuana can then be sold by celebrity spokespersons as a product; a product of a particular truth brand. Medicalization, as a process, is a commodity. It enters into the mass-minded public market as hip, stylish, compassionate, new and even exciting. Pro-medicalization sentiment transmits through public relations marketing campaigns. The idea of medical marijuana may then become a sound bite or a product for an individual to appropriate and internalize as an accessory to accentuate an already attractive and progressive personality or image.

Comported out of the *Just Say No* fashion of thought into the newest *Just Say Know* fad, an individual first buys into the latest brand of truth about marijuana. Therefore, the criminalization of marijuana discourse moves out of vogue as the newer medicalization of marijuana discourse moves into vogue. The newest brand of truth may then become desirable for mass consumption, for it is a marker of the most recent and current fashion of thought. Consequently, the newest truth brand manifests itself as a symbol by which the new coercive discursive entity may find a semi-permanent location in space and time.

Cultural transformation may be simply an outcome of the prolonged and massive marketing of a particular truth brand. As a result, the newest industry of statement production may then distribute specific products tailor-made for mass consumption. Citizens then prepare themselves for new paradigm insemination. For example, crude market advertising mechanisms of market cool can sell anti-prohibition culture. Through external and visible symbiosis, (such as shirts, videos, DVDs, celebrities, and gatherings), likeminded and progressive people are encouraged to connect with other likeminded and progressive people. Examples of the anti-drug war material products currently available for purchase and consumption are too numerous to itemize.

The commoditization of cultural rebellion is nothing new within the context of developed western capitalism. Even so, the commoditization of incremental public policy productions associated with reforming our nations existing policies of drug prohibition are worthy of mention. These commodities of reform connect individuals participating in medicinal marijuana campaigns as they share common experiences as a reform community. Here, citizens idealize the common experience, violation by an oppressive police state which still engages in old guard cultural protectionism (i.e., marijuana prohibition). Within this context, medical marijuana activists identify marijuana prohibitionists (i.e., law enforcement) as the other and recast them as a threat to the reform group members' well being. Consequently, the marijuana reform community becomes more cohesive and powerful as new horror stories about the evils of the anti-drug crusades are told and retold, produced, and reproduced. It is their persecution by law enforcement, which fuels their collective quest for marijuana policy reform.

Through their collective experiential knowledge base, the individuals of the marijuana reform community provide testimonies to one another. As a result, they are emphatically able to illustrate how they all, at one time or another, have been on the other side of the intensely powerful and overly coercive anti-drug discursive complex. Stories of how the other (i.e., anti-drug law enforcement agents) attempted to demonize their humanity, at one point in time or another, are told and retold. A collective form of mass victimization is holistically and individually experienced as the moral imperative to decriminalize marijuana solidifies within each member of the reform community. These non-profit anti-prohibition storytellers may then be perceived by the reform group as authentic activists working to end America's longest war (i.e., America's drug war), a war waged against America's moral citizens by America's immoral citizens. As a result, charismatic leaders may surface as articulate and persuasive storytellers. These reform storytellers have found a contemporary collective and a powerful voice in their quest to decriminalize marijuana. The once-silenced voices have banded together and are now loud enough for lawmakers to hear. As a result, they are now developing into the newest industry of drug policy truth. These voices have articulated a new and influential superstructure of anti-prohibition knowledge, politically charged with medical science and a new moral purpose.

The newest industry of marijuana medicalization predictably produces new information products, quickly heralded as innovative "truths." Consequently, the discursive machinery of medicalization facilitates the creation, emergence and proliferation of the nation's newest framework for regulating the behavior of marijuana consumers. The newest model for social control receives the billing of therapeutic, gentle, and supportive. With respect to marijuana using proclivities, citizen regulation may no longer be primarily physically coercive. The newest coercive discourse (i.e., medicalization) need not even pursue its fodder (i.e., its patients). For the newest model of control, individuals may willingly line up to receive professional chemical adjustment advice (i.e., prescriptions). To maximize the economic efficiency associated with this new form of state sanctioned subjectivity, individuals may be encouraged to finance their own treatment and care.

Medicalization is less obvious, less crass and less brutish than criminalization. Medicalization is technologically advanced, internal, and economical. Medicalized individuals are often (but not always) willing, non-combative, and intellectually and emotionally invested in their treatment. Once again, the populace is encouraged to believe in the benevolence of medical science. At the same time, if the populace continues to be plagued with prohibition disenchantment, the lay population may keep on questioning the efficacy of America's correctional industrial complex, and the warehousing of human beings and human potential. Simultaneously, the growth of the already massive medical industrial complex becomes unfettered.

Chapter Six

Conclusions

Linking Discourse and Consequence in Historical Context

This book introduced the social history of marijuana in America from 1906 to 2004. Consequently, two deviant designations associated with past and present drug policy debates became the central objects of investigation. As a result, I demonstrated that the way by which Americans view this plant has altered dramatically over the past century. I also examined some of the public policy implications of applying these moral paradigms to the regulatory efforts associated with marijuana. Unfortunately, most do not understand marijuana to be anything other than a crime or a medicine. Implicit in these two competing ways of understanding, is an often unspoken accident of history, lacking in neither scope nor drama. My ultimate goal was to uncover evidence of such a historical accident in an effort to understand the many different conditions under which marijuana prohibition originated. Consequently, I furthered understanding of the many different conditions that may influence the eventual success or failure of today's efforts to medicalize marijuana.

As previously mentioned, my study was informed by a strict social constructionist position (i.e., substances such as marijuana do not exist outside of their socially constructed definitions and meanings). Throughout the work, I viewed marijuana by using many different definitions at the same time (i.e., a plant, medicine, crime, and industrial product). Simultaneously, I did not view marijuana as anything tangible at all (i.e., not a plant, medicine, or industrial product). I viewed marijuana as strictly a social construct, nothing else. In any case, I observed marijuana as nothing more and nothing less than what social processes construct marijuana to be.

I drew on guidance from sociological, criminological, and postmodern theorists; namely, Peter Conrad, Joseph Schneider, Michel Foucault, and Elliot Currie. With these past theoretical contributions guiding my historical investigation, a qualitative method, provided by Kendall and Wickham, proved to be indispensable. Through utilizing their interpretation of Foucault's analytical method for analyzing specific histories, I addressed some of the topics associated with America's contemporary medicinal marijuana debate.

My research efforts were unique because my line of investigation focused on better understanding processes that depict how societal members interpret marijuana and some of the information that often accompanies the plant. Individuals or groups were not the units of my analysis, statements were. As a researcher, I was not interested in the validity or invalidity of the truth claims associated with each side of pro/con marijuana debate. My investigation described how these processes serve to extend the power of the government to regulate the behavior of its citizens. Whether or not these processes intentionally or unintentionally entered into play, to extend the power of state and federal authorities, was inconsequential to the success of my research.

Using Kendall and Wickham's specific method of Foucault's Archaeology, I examined the form of discourse associated with criminalization, which Conrad and Schneider predicted I would find. This required that I disinter or dig up statements associated with past federal legislative initiatives, which criminalized marijuana from 1906 to 1988. By this method, I provided data or documentation that the prohibition of the plant *Cannabis Sativa* was the practical result of this discourse's origin and growth; as were the consequences associated with criminalizing such behaviors. As a significant, yet unexpected outcome, I tied together discourse and consequence in historical context. After conducting the Archaeology of marijuana criminalization, I depicted the competing discourse of medicalization in its vital and emergent state.

Using Kendall and Wickham's specific method of Foucault's Genealogy, I placed the discursive phenomenon of marijuana medicalization within a contemporary historical period dating from 1996 to 2004. At first, the two forms of discourse (i.e., criminalization and medicalization) seemed distinctive and oppositional. Through a comparison of them, however, I demonstrated that they are nearly identical in form and share an unreflective view of the legitimate use of coercive governmental power to regulate marijuana.

Conrad and Schneider's five-stage sequential theoretical model, once generalized, revealed the characteristics and nature of both discursive processes to be identical in form. Using Kendall and Wickham's method, my research uncovered evidence of the ways that deviant designations apply to marijuana and its users. Consequently, I produced an analysis that supports Conrad and Schneider's theoretical assertions. In addition, I discussed how these designations became popular among other possible designations (i.e., herbal remedy or industrial hemp).

Additionally, I concluded that both discourses about marijuana serve to obviate any discussion of the constitutional or unconstitutional nature of anti-drug legislation in America. While the highly polarized political pitch associated with the pro/con marijuana debate provides for fascinating subject matter to investigate, such a hostile political climate discourages politically unbiased researchers from acquiring much needed data on the validity and reliability of claims made about marijuana's medicinal or criminogenic properties.

Medical marijuana is a contemporary topic with a high public profile, and mainstream news sources often write about the plant and the nation's effort to prohibit or regulate it. Even so, I assert that my analysis of shifting labels as they apply to marijuana users is unique and significant. At the same time, I contend that my analysis is not overreaching in etiological scope. In my treatment of discursive processes, I described how some deviant designations change over time and become historically specific. By my assertion that some deviant designations (such as witches or communists) are historically specific, I mean that some deviant designations can only emerge during specific times and in specific places throughout history.

In addition, I noted the truth claims of each process, and emphasized how accidental occurrences often provided opportunities for the legitimization of the processes themselves. As mentioned above, the scientific validity of such truth claims was not a key concern of my analysis. Consequently, the ways that deviant designations come and go, succeed or fail, fade or endure, were of utmost importance to my research. To further my understanding of these processes and, consequently, the way by which marijuana was/is socially constructed, I utilized particular statements as windows through which I observe and document the exercise of power and its employee, knowledge.

Using eclectic sources, my study documented how two different discursive processes work in similar ways. In a daunting effort, I examined statements generated from state and federal legislative initiatives and the outcomes associated with their passage. I narrated high profile court cases and the people who drove them through the nation's legal system. I scrutinized transcripts of legislative hearings, congressional debates, speeches, as well as select committee and subcommittee minutes. I read reports from Washington based non-profit organizations along with major newspaper articles and editorials. Periodical and professional journals, newsletters, pamphlets, and even emails and on-line postings were surveyed. In addition, I sorted through and examined letters of solicitation and public memorandums, as well as other amateur and professional literature associated with these two processes. I did so because my method required me to use an opportunistic approach to data collection and analysis. As a result, I gained an appreciation of the scope and drama associated with the documentation that I collected and analyzed. At times, the contents of my data archive were surprising.

Currently, innovative drug policy reformers do not regard the medicinal marijuana movement as the cutting edge of drug policy reform in America. However, because of the movement's ties with institutional legitimacy (i.e., medicine and deep-pocketed backers), it enjoys a high profile in debate forums from popular to academic. By describing current efforts to medicalize marijuana within the context of the history of marijuana criminalization, I was able to deliver a more balanced view of today's popular social movement to medicalize marijuana.

The Method: Assessing Utility

I utilized the Archaeology of marijuana criminalization and the Genealogy of marijuana medicalization alongside one another to examine three different sets of influential events. I observed these sets in an effort to uncover evidence that could further an understanding of how two official deviant designations historically associated with marijuana emerged and became proliferate.

The first set I examined with the Archaeology was composed of eight federal acts that served to make possible the federal prohibition of marijuana from 1906 to 1988. The second set I examined with the Genealogy was associated with the actions of the first nine states to legitimize medical marijuana from 1996 to 2004. I also examined the third set with the Genealogy. This set was composed of three recent high profile legal disputes that took place on the national stage. These three cases helped to clarify federal authority to prohibit medicinal marijuana use in states that have decriminalized the medical use of marijuana.

I used the events within these sets to locate potential discursive processes at work. Each event generated a plethora of statements, which underwent analysis. Through the collection and analysis of these statements, or data, I was able to observe and describe the structures that Conrad and Schneider's medicalization theory predicted I would find; as well as the interactional dynamics that created and sustained each discursive process.

Federal law outlaws the plant because federal law defines marijuana as a drug with no medical value, under any circumstance. As a result, any existing or future state law that decriminalizes the medicinal use of the plant has been and remains unstable. Therefore, I devoted attention to the origins of these federal powers through using the Archaeology to investigate relevant data in connection to the first set. While the Archaeology attended to the first data set, the Genealogy attended to the second and third sets of data.

The Genealogy examined the second set to collect and examine data associated with the disjunction between state and federal laws over the medicinal use of marijuana. In addition, the Genealogy examined the third set to collect and examine data associated with moral entrepreneurs seeking to defend or gain the administrative turf associated with the regulation of marijuana. By using the nation's courts to voice their respective positions, these claims makers continually delivered public statements as they battled to legitimize their own claims. In this manner, they concomitantly de-legitimized their adversaries' claims. Consequently, the Genealogy documented some of the tactics used to pursue discursive sovereignty, institutionalize legitimacy and semi-permanency through legislative anchoring.

By utilizing Kendall and Wickham's method, I presented past and present social histories of marijuana. Moreover, I demonstrated how legitimate uses of marijuana have changed over time. In addition, I alluded to the idea that continual change is more likely than not. By examining the process of marijuana medicalization through the employment of the Genealogy, I historically couched today's medical marijuana controversy in a larger political conflict between social constructions of crime and illness.

Modifying, Utilizing, and Building Upon Medicalization Theory

By examining the past process of marijuana criminalization through the Archaeology as well as the present process of marijuana medicalization through the Genealogy, I demonstrated the utility, versatility and power of a slightly modified version of medicalization theory. Once I adapted or generalized medicalization theory to be applicable to both processes of deviant designation change, the methodological device consistently and dependably put forth evidence validating Conrad and Schneider's theoretical framework.

Implicitly integrating a slightly generalized version of medicalization theory (Conrad and Schneider, 1992) and a new qualitative methodology (Kendall and Wickham, 2000) into an analytic framework that depicts, explains and understands how new discursive processes predictably emerge, was not accomplished easily. Linking perspective gained from identifying how discursive processes originate new designations to perspective gained from identifying how discursive processes sustain recently established designations, involved connecting Conrad and Schneider's theoretical tenets with the five theoretical principles of Foucault's Science of Discipline.

To date, marijuana has remained illegal largely because its criminal designation has undergone institutionalization in America's numerous county, state and federal bureaucracies. These large institutions charged with educating, healing, protecting, and punishing American citizens continually reaffirm the reality that those producing, possessing, distributing, or using marijuana are criminals. As the Archaeology demonstrated, the past process that criminalized marijuana altered the border line between normal and abnormal to where it is today. Hence, almost all of what Americans officially now know about marijuana, was influenced or created by the discursive process that accentuated the adverse mental and physical health consequences of using marijuana under any circumstance. Consequently, successful political and fiscal claim makers used official information or knowledge derived from the past discursive process of marijuana criminalization to advance specific agendas, acquiring more administrative turf while also gaining budgetary priority. Their claims slowly transformed into institutionalized and unquestioned facts about marijuana.

Next, I linked perspective gained from five of Foucault's theoretical principles, of how discursive processes sustain the designations they produce, with perspective gained from Elliot Currie. Currie's theoretical contribution identified how, under rare historically specific circumstances, mechanisms of social control can begin to enter into modes of hyper-production. Hence, I connected the five principles of Foucault's Science of Discipline with the four theoretical characteristics given by Elliot Currie. By describing why some criminal designations undergo hyperactive reproduction while others do not, Currie's tenets guided my research as the Archaeology examined the later decades of marijuana criminalization.

Currie's four theoretical generalizations furthered understanding of what social control characteristics are often associated with the emergence of "an enormously effective machine for the systematic and massive production of confessed deviants" (Currie, 1968: 351). During the later stages of the Archaeology, I marshal evidence supporting Currie's conceptual framework. During the 1980s, a high degree of structural interest was observable by criminal justice agencies charged with apprehending and convicting marijuana criminals. Criminal justice agencies charged with enforcing marijuana prohibition held extraordinary powers for suppressing marijuana use rates. Moreover, while lacking internal mechanisms of restraint, many of these law enforcement agencies displayed invulnerability to external mechanisms of restraint from other social institutions; traditionally charged with overseeing issues associated with the public's health and welfare. The Archaeology demonstrated evidence supporting the assertion that the war on drugs facilitated overzealous attempts to pursue and ceremoniously label marijuana users as criminals. As an unintended consequence, the extreme criminalization of marijuana set the stage for the emergence of the medicinal marijuana movement. Hence, the end of the Archaeology served to introduce the Genealogy of marijuana medicalization.

The Genealogy contributed to an understanding of the current medicalization process. It showed how the medical model has been in play to transform state policy regarding the prohibition of marijuana, thus putting federal lawmakers on the defensive. The Genealogy also emphasized how nine states implemented the medicalization paradigm as an appropriate way to respond to regulating marijuana use. The Genealogy demonstrated medicalization to be consistent with the therapeutic state model of citizen behavior regulation; much in the same way that criminalization was demonstrated, by the Archaeology, to be consistent with the paternalistic state model of behavior regulation.

I illustrated that state-level medical marijuana legislation was an attempt to use the therapeutic state apparatus of soft power to temper or reform a systematic over reliance on hard power to regulate marijuana. Both analyses portrayed the active and systematic regulation of marijuana as the shared goal of both sides of the medical marijuana debate. As a result, the Genealogy was able to marshal evidence asserting that both processes of medicalization and criminalization are structurally similar mechanisms for identifying, defining, and altering social problems, satiating a governmental need to regulate the behavior of some of its citizens (Conrad and Schneider, 1992: 227-288).

Both discursive processes produce intended as well as unintended consequences. Each definition, crime or medicine, represents popular attempts to regulate the behavior of citizens. In addition, both sides of the debate are unlikely to consider alternatives that fall outside state and federal spheres of power and authority. The right of law abiding adult citizens to make their own well informed, or ill informed, decisions about what they choose to ingest into their own bodies, or grow on their own land, is not presently on the table for debate. Consequently, responsible self-regulated drug use is not an option for those interested in using marijuana to treat illnesses.

Decriminalizing moderate recreational marijuana use, which often takes place within responsible settings among consenting adults, is not debatable within the present political climate. Even though responsible recreational marijuana use may not be very different from the responsible use of alcohol, public policy debate allowing recreational use is a long way from entering into the mainstream. Quite simply, like alcohol, marijuana use may be moderate or excessive.

The Moral and Legal Implications of Medicalizing Marijuana

Conrad and Schneider left social scientists a theoretical map of the sociological landscape as it pertains to the medical marijuana social movement. Through meticulously detailing how badness can transform into sickness, they provided insight into some of the societal costs and benefits that might result from medicalizing marijuana use. Medicalization theory illustrates how the development of institutional resources and public facilities to treat illness becomes a moral obligation for all citizens. As a result, using the medical model (instead of the criminal model) to regulate marijuana carries fewer connotations of immorality, low self-control, or defects of character for those who choose to use marijuana. Nevertheless, medicalizing marijuana is not without problematic and unexpected outcomes.

In their eagerness to choose the lesser of two public policy evils, Americans run the risk of failing to consider the availability of alternatives. What is normal to today's public is normal because it is what they have come to regularly experience throughout their daily lives. Laypersons might view their present condition, which envelops them, and erroneously assume that things have always been the way they are now. What is normal now may not have been normal a century ago.

Governmental regulation of marijuana, through criminalization or medicalization, has not always been so intrusive. Thomas Szasz (1974: vii) once stated, "If a hundred years ago, the American government had tried to regulate what substances its citizens could or could not digest, the effort would have been ridiculed as absurd and rejected as unconstitutional." Today many fail to see the strangeness in government boldly asserting an unquestioned form of absolute authority over what citizens choose to ingest into their own private property (i.e., their bodies) or grow on their own private land. David Musto (1973: 247) asked an important and currently unanswered question in his now seminal work, *The American Disease: Origins of Narcotic Control*:

> Why did the Supreme Court agree that a federal statute could outlaw narcotics, when the Constitution itself had to be amended to outlaw alcohol? One answer to this may be that in the case of narcotics the consensus was almost absolute; everyone appeared to agree on the evils of these drugs. For alcohol, there was no such agreement.

Today, as demonstrated by the recent success of the medical marijuana movement, there is no such agreement about marijuana and the constitutionality of prohibiting marijuana without first amending the U.S. Constitution may receive debate.

Medicalization theory indirectly warns that the process of medicalization runs the risk of turning users of marijuana into technical objects, delivering users into the hands of institutional experts whose goal is the rehabilitation of the user (Conrad and Schneider 1992: 277-288). This process empowers experts and medical professionals as agents of social control. As Szasz (1974: xiii) stated more than thirty years ago, "Perhaps such preying of people upon people - such symbolic cannibalism, providing meaning for one life by depriving another of meaning - is an inexorable part of the human condition and is therefore inevitable." Indeed, for Foucault, such a system of domination and submission is the very basis of our social order.

Within the unequal distribution of social capital among Americans, the framed medical marijuana debate is emerging into public view as a powerful and "healthy" form of conflict, whereby, different groups representing different interests, values and beliefs clash for power and authority. Missed, by design, in this conflagration are the established and unquestioned senses of governmental authority as therapeutic and/or paternalistic, as an infantilized citizenry is benevolently cared for and stunted.

I debunk the discursive process of medicalizing marijuana, pointing out that the criminalization of marijuana was an ill-conceived construct, in much the same way that the medicalization of marijuana is an ill-conceived construct. As I suspend my research efforts, I contend that marijuana use is no more a crime than it is a medicine. Marijuana is a plant, that when ingested may produce a range of temporary affects from euphoria to paranoia, much of which depends on the social setting in which the drug is used.

In my comparison of discursive processes, I show that the contemporary success associated with the medicalization of marijuana is inextricable to the way medicalization undermines the authority of the criminal justice system. However, the medical model itself has not escaped criticism. I posed questions about the legitimacy of the model, and its authority and scientific objectivity. Conrad and Schneider suggest that the process of medicalization depoliticizes marijuana use. Criminals become patients under the process, but their condition of control changes little. In popular idiom, meet the new boss, same as the old boss.

Conclusion

Finally, I conclude that a continuum exists where illness is at one end and preference at the other. Here, the medicalization of marijuana assures that the ill are not labeled criminal but obscures us from recognizing that the adult individual can make his or her own well-informed decisions. The resultant infantilized adult, who once chose to ingest or not to ingest the substance, is now a stranger to his/her own agency to exercise his/her own freedom responsibly; or to suffer the consequences of his/her own foolish designs. The institutionalized use of the label or category of ill commands institutional support and technical know how. However, governmental authorities forfeit the freedom and liberty of citizens as payment for paternalistic/ therapeutic services rendered. Consequently, one generation not only mortgages their own freedoms, but the autonomy and freedom of many generations to come.

At its core, the public debate over medical marijuana's legitimacy grapples with the choice to accept or reject the medical model and its application to behavior currently labeled criminal (Conrad and Schneider, 1992: 277-288). As this debate intensifies, the unintended consequences associated with medicalizing marijuana may continue to avoid scholarly and popular attention. Taken as a whole, I modified a version of medicalization theory to help illustrate that marijuana prohibition has a relatively short social history, and, by implication, that marijuana medicalization is still in its formative stages.

An understanding of any social problem requires historical analysis and I began my inquiry with the past history of marijuana criminalization. Placing a social problem in historical context promotes a relative interpretation of the problem. I also furthered understanding of how the official response to a social problem in one area creates new problems in other areas. Consequently, my research offered social histories of two discursive processes placed side by side. By using far ranging documentation, in order to entertain alternative possibilities that I realized outside of existing frames, my study demonstrated that what Americans know about marijuana was and continues to be under social construction, by highly skilled claims makers on both sides of the debate. I explicated how these claims serve as a base for informed decisions and scientifically grounded discourse, by exhuming past and present histories about marijuana and delineated the construction of policy and the consequences of practice.

Using medicalization theory, and Kendall and Wickham's specific Foucaultian method, I constructed a social history of marijuana, which was (and still is) dramatic. Today, the stakes are as high as they ever were, as these processual adversaries battle once again for supremacy and status quo representation. Clearly, both processes of criminalization and medicalization have far-reaching and profound implications for everyday life in America.

My histories demonstrate that competing discourses about marijuana are complex, linked to the exercise of power and power's selective employment of "knowledge". When I stripped away the accoutrements of human interaction, nothing more than a simple plant was uncloaked. Understanding these official inventions was, in fact, the primary undertaking of my intellectual pilgrimage. However, recognizing the very real consequences of marijuana prohibition and medicalization was of import. Be they intentional or unintentional, such consequences transform fictitious official designations of deviance. As they do so, I cannot emphasize enough the importance of reflexivity as deviant designations undergo change and transformation.

At present, I cannot answer questions of whether or not medicalization produces a more complete, yet subtle, exercise of power than criminalization. Nevertheless, the assumption that medicalization is a less intrusive framework for the exercise of governmental authority should not be embraced. While criminalization is as crass as it is obvious, it is at least transparent in its application. Governmental regulation of the chemical content of citizens' bodies/minds promises to free all from intemperate inclinations, yet delivers neither freedom nor temperance. As an important aside, Szasz (1974: 160, 180) reminds us that today's social problem may be tomorrow's example of ill-conceived public policy Comstockery.

> One of the gravest psychiatric concerns in the nineteenth century was masturbation; and one of the most serious mental diseases was the madness that it caused, namely 'masturbatory insanity'...The 'danger' of masturbation disappeared when we ceased to believe in it: we then ceased to attribute danger to the practice and to its practitioners; and ceased to call it 'self abuse'...Of course some people still behave in disagreeable and even dangerous ways, but we no longer attribute their behavior to masturbation or self abuse: we now attribute their behavior to self-medication or drug abuse.

In keeping with Szasz's emphatic example, I argue that the danger associated with marijuana is external to the drug itself. The danger associated with "masturbation insanity" or "self-abuse" did not disappear because of history. The "danger" associated with "masturbatory insanity" disappeared because social discourse about masturbation changed. A new social discourse emerged about masturbation and destroyed collectively held notions of masturbatory "self-abuse" along with the masturbation social problem. Rather than erroneously redefining a crime into a medicine, Americans should consider regulating marijuana much in the same way that they regulate tobacco: decriminalized for adults yet officially discouraged.

To use or not use marijuana is a choice. It is not a crime or a medicine but a plant, and a weed at that. I argue that the danger associated with marijuana will no longer exist when Americans cease to engage in and believe social discourse that frames marijuana as dangerous. Only by first ceasing to define the plant as a pathogen or as a panacea, may citizens succeed in accurately re-defining the plant as a plant and nothing more. Consequently, those who use the plant for whatever reason may be better understood for what they are: social actors exercising their freedom of choice, responsibly or irresponsibly. Having said as much, the solution to the marijuana problem hides behind the official acknowledgment that marijuana is not and has never been the problem; while America's domestic obsession with prohibiting or regulating the plant (along with those who use it) is and has always been the problem. In closing, I quote Thomas Szasz (1974: 154) as he emphasizes the fact that there are only two ways to control human behavior, "by the person...through self control; or by another person (or group), through coercion. *Tertium non datur*; there is no third way."

Bibliography

Albert, Tanya. 2002. "Court to decide what doctors can say about medical marijuana." *A.M. News. Garberville Pot Dispatch.* May 27. Retrieved March 5, 2005 (www.digthatcrazyfarout.com/gpd/-GvillePD1027.htm).

Anslinger, H.J., and Tompkins, W.F. 1953. *The Traffic in Narcotics.* United States: Funk & Wagnalls, Company.

Baum, Dan. 1996. *Smoke and Mirrors: The War on Drugs and the Politics of Failure.* New York NY: Little, Brown and Company.

Becker, H. 1963. *Outsiders: Studies in the Sociology of Deviance.* New York NY: Free Press.

Bergman, L., Levis, K., Hamilton, D. and Oriana Zill. 2000. "Drug Wars: Part Two" Retrieved March 30, 2006 (http://www.pbs.org/wgbh/pages/frontline/shows/drugs/ etc/transcript2.html).

Bikel, Ofra. 1999. "Snitch." OPTV: Frontline Snitch: #1709. Retrieved July 1, 2004 (http://www.pbs.org/wgbh/pages/frontline/shows/snitch/etc/script.html).

Bonnie, R., and Whitebread, C. H. 1970. The Forbidden Fruit and The Tree of Knowledge: An Inquiry into the Legal History of American Marijuana Prohibition. *Virginia Law Review.* Vol.56, Num.6.

Brooke, James. 1998. "States Vote Medical Use of Marijuana." *The New York Times*, November 5, B10.

Carpiano, Richard. 2001. "Passive Medicalization: The Case of Viagra and Erectile Dysfunction." *Sociological Spectrum.* Vol. 21, num. 3, Pg. 441-450.

Congressional Record. 1935. Congressional Record-Senate 05 03 1935. "The Narcotic Drug Evil." Retrieved June 11, 2004, (http://www.onlinepot.org/reefermadness/congressmarch1935b.htm).

Congressional Record. 1935. Congressional Record-Senate 29 03 1935. "World Narcotic Defense Association Addresses." Retrieved June 11, 2004 (http://www.onlinepot.org/reefermadness/congressmarch1935.htm).

Conrad, Peter. 1992. "Medicalization and Social Control." *Annual Review of Sociology.* 18: 209-232.

Conrad, Peter and Joseph Schneider. 1992. *Deviance and Medicalization: From Badness to Sickness.* Philadelphia: Temple University Press.

CSDP. 2002. CSDP Research Report. Nixon Tapes Show Roots of Marijuana Prohibition: 06 July 2004 <http://www.csdp.org/research/shafernixon.pdf>.

Currie, E. P. 1968. "Crimes without Criminals: Witchcraft and Its Control in Renaissance Europe." *Law & Society Review.* 3, no. 1 (1968): 7-32. Reprinted as chap. 19 in *The Social Organization of Law.* Edited by Donald Black. New York: Seminar Press, 1973, pp. 344-367.

DEA. 2004. Online History of DEA.1970 - 1979. Retrieved July 6, 2004 (http://www.usdoj.gov/dea/pubs/history/deahistory_01.htm#5).

Duke, Steven B. and Albert C. Gross. 1993. *America's Longest War: Rethinking Our Tragic Crusade against Drugs.* New York: G. P. Putnam's Sons.

Dworkin, Ronald. 2001. "The Medicalization of Unhappiness." *The Public Interest.* Vol. 144, Pg. 85-99.

FBI. 2003. "Crime in the United States 2002." *Uniform Crime Reports, 2002.* U.S. Department of Justice. Federal Bureau of Investigation. (For more information, please see: www.fbi.gov).

FDA. 2004. Federal Food and Drug Act of 1906 (The "Wiley Act"). U.S. Food and Drug Administration. Public Law Num. 59-384, 34 Stat. 768 (1906), 21 U.S.C. Sec 1-15 (1934), (Repealed in 1938 by 21 U.S.C. Sec 329 (a)).

Fillingham, Lydia Alix. 1993. *Foucault for Beginners.* New York NY: Writers and Readers. Publishing , Inc.

Foucault, M. 1972. *The Archaeology of Knowledge.* New York: Pantheon books

Foucault, M. 1977. *Power/knowledge.* New York: Pantheon. In Seidman, S. (ed.) *The Postmodern Turn: New Perspectives on Social theory.* Cambridge, MA: Cambridge University Press.

Foucault, M. 1978. *The History of Sexuality: Volume 1: An introduction.* New York: Vintage Books.

Foucault, M. 1980. "Two Lectures." In Gordon, C. (ed.) *Michel Foucault. Power/Knowledge: Selected Interviews and Other Writings* 1972-1977. Brighton: Harvester.

Foucault, M. 1984. "What is Enlightenment?" In Rainbow, P. (ed.) *The Foucault Reader*. New York: Pantheon.

Foucault, M. 1988. "The Art of Telling the Truth." In Kritzman, L.D. (ed.) *Michel Foucault. Politics, Philosophy, Culture: Interviews and Other Writings of Michel Foucault*, 1977-1984. New York: Routledge.

Gieringer, Dale. 1999. "The Forgotten Origins of Cannabis Prohibition in California." *Journal of Contemporary Drug Problems*, Summer 1999 26 (2): Pp. 236-288.

Gillies, Val. 2000. "Young People and Family Life: Analyzing and Comparing Disciplinary Discourses." *Journal of Youth Studies*. Vol. 3, num. 2, Pg. 211-228.

Goldberg, Carey. 2000. "Maine Sees Medical Use for Its Seized Marijuana." *The New York Times*, March 14, A16.

Goode, Erich. 2005. *Drugs in American Society*. New York: Phillip A. Butcher.

Herer, Jack. 1985. *The Emperor Wears No Clothes*. Van Nuys, CA: HEMP Publishing.

Jones, Shaina. 2003. "Justices Consider Medical Marijuana Laws." *Legal Times*. October 12. Retrieved March 3, 2005 (http://cannabisnews.com/news).

Kampia, R. 2004. Information derived from an email soliciting contributions for the Marijuana Policy Project Foundation. P.O. Box 77492 Capitol Hill Washington, D.C. 20013. (Please see: http://www.MarijuanaPolicy.org)

Kendall, Gavin, and Gary Wickham. 2000. *Using Foucault's Methods*. Thousand Oaks CA: SAGE Productions Ltd.

King, Rufus. 1972. "The Drug Hang Up, America's Fifty-Year Folly." *Schaffer Library of Policy*. Retrieved June 21, 2004 (http://www.druglibrary. org/special/king/ – dhu/dhu-16.htm).

Lee, Stephen. 2004. *Newsaic*. "Medical Marijuana." Retrieved March 3, 2005 (http://www.newsaic.com/mwdrugs.html).

Lloyd, Gwynedd and Claire Norris. 1999. "Including ADHD?" *Disability and Society*. Vol. 14, num. 4, Pg. 505-517.

Marx, Karl. 1963. *The 18th Brumaire of Louis Bonaparte*. New York: International Publishers (Original work published in 1852).

McCoy, Alfred. 2004. "A Quick History of Opium." Retrieved. June 12, 2004 (http://www.a1b2c3.com/drugs/opi002.htm).

Megill, A. 1985. *Prophets of Extremity: Nietzsche, Heidegger, Foucault, Derrida.* Berkeley: University of California Press.

Mills, Sarah. 2003. *Michel Foucault.* London: Rutledge.

Molotsky, Irvin. 1999. "Washington Backs Medical Use of Marijuana." *The New York Times*, September 21, A27.

MPP. 2004. Information derived from a letter soliciting contributions for the Marijuana Policy Project Foundation. P.O. Box 77492 Capitol Hill Washington D.C. 20013. (Please see: http://www.MarijuanaPolicy.org)

Musto, D. F. 1973. *The American Disease: Origins of Narcotic Control.* New Haven: Yale University Press.

NORML. 2005. "State by State Laws." Retrieved on March 6 (http://www.norml.org/-index.cfm?Group_ID=4516).

NYT. 1937. "World Group to Push Fight on Marijuana." *The New York Times.* Retrieved on July 9, 2004. (http://www.druglibrary.org/schaffer/hemp/history/nytimes/022137.htm).

ONDCP. 2004. *Strategizer 44: Marijuana-Debunking the Myths*. A Series of Technical Assistance Manuals for Community Coalitions. Alexandra VA: Community Ant-Drug Coalitions of America.

Pollan, Michael. 1997. "Living with Medical Marijuana." *The New York Times*, July 20, E23.

Putnam, T. 2004. *DARE Graduates Vow to be Drug Free.* The Carthage Press. 03-26-04. Vol. 120, Num. 73:1A.

Rafalovich, Adam. 2001. "The Conceptual History of Attention Deficit Hyperactivity Disorder: Idiocy, Imbecility, Encephalitis and the Child Deviant, 1877-1929." *Deviant Behavior*. Vol. 22, num. 2, Pg. 93-115.

Reiman, Jeffrey. 2004. *The Rich Get Richer and the Poor Get Prison: Ideology, Class, and Criminal Justice.* Boston. Allyn and Bacon.

Riska, Elianne. 2000. "The Rise and Fall of Type A Man." *Social Science and Medicine.* Vol. 51, num. 11, Pg. 1665-1674.

Rossol, Josh. 2001. "The Medicalization of Deviance as an Interactive Achievement: The Construction of Compulsive Gambling." *Symbolic Interactionism.* Vol. 24, num. 3, Pg. 315-341.

Schaffer Library of Drug Policy. 2004. "Harrison Narcotics Tax Act, 1914." Retrieved May 31, 2004 (http://www.druglibrary.org/schaffer/history/e1910/harrisonact.htm).

Schram, Sanford. 2000. "In the Clinic: The Medicalization of Welfare." *Social Text.* Vol. 18, num. 1(62), Pg. 81-107.

Shelden, R. and William B. Brown. 2003. *Criminal Justice in America: A Critical View.* Boston: Allyn & Bacon

Speaker, S. 2001. "The Struggle of Mankind Against its Deadliest Foe: Themes of Counter-Subversion in Anti-Narcotic Campaigns, 1920-1940." *Journal of Social History.* Spring 2001, Vol.34: Num.3.

Sterngold, James. 2000. "Hawaii Lawmakers Approve Bill On Medical Use of Marijuana." *The New York Times*, April 26, A14.

Szasz, Thomas. 1974. *Ceremonial Chemistry: The Ritual Persecution of Drugs, Addicts, and Pushers.* New York: Anchor Press/Doubleday.

Szasz, Thomas. 1992. *Our Right to Drugs: The Case for a Free Market.* New York: Praeger.

U.S. Department of Justice. 2005. "DEA Staffing and Appropriations FY 1972-2005." DEA Staffing and Budget. Retrieved on May 12 (www.usdoj.gov/dea/agency-/staffing.htm).

Walter, Tony. 2000. "Grief Narratives: The Role of Medicine in the Policing of Grief." *Anthropology and Medicine.* Vol. 7, num. 1, Pg. 97-114.

Wellman, David. 2000. "From Evil to Illness: Medicalizing Racism." *American Journal of Orthopsychiatry.* Vol. 70, num. 1, Pg. 28-32.

Zimmer, L and Jon Morgan. 1997. *Marijuana Myths and facts: A review of the Scientific Evidence.* New York. The Lindesmith Center.

Index

Jeffrey M. London

Dr. Jeffrey M. London is an Assistant Professor in the Department of Criminal Justice and Criminology, the School of Professional Studies, at Metropolitan State College of Denver in Colorado. Dr. London received his Ph.D. in Sociology from the University of Colorado at Boulder.